# *YOU*

## *Are the Adventure!*

*By*

J. ALLEN BOONE

*New York*

PRENTICE-HALL, INC.

TO

# LILLIAN GIBBS BOONE

A LOVELY, FRAGRANT RHODE ISLAND GENTLEWOMAN
WHO DID ME THE GREAT HONOR AND FAVOR
OF BEING MY MOTHER

# CONTENTS

1. EXPLORER'S ITCH . . . . . . . . 1

2. THE ANCIENT GESTURE . . . . . . 9

3. THUMBS UP! . . . . . . . . . 17

4. HELL-DIVERS . . . . . . . . . 25

5. ADVENTURERS . . . . . . . . . 32

6. SUPERVAGABOND . . . . . . . . 39

7. RHYTHM . . . . . . . . . 46

8. VERITIES . . . . . . . . . . 54

9. REFORMERS . . . . . . . . . 62

10. ROCKING CHAIRS . . . . . . . . 69

11. BEING . . . . . . . . . . 77

12. BUGGING AROUND . . . . . . . 84

13. ENCIRCLEMENTS . . . . . . . . 91

14. MARGINS . . . . . . . . . 99

15. SCAPEGOATS . . . . . . . . 108

16. YOU and YOU! . . . . . . . . 115

17. PRACTICE FLIGHT . . . . . . . 121

18. MEET "A BIGGIE!" . . . . . . . 128

19. DILEMMA . . . . . . . . . 136

20. IN-AND-OUTER . . . . . . . . 144

[v]

# CONTENTS

21. OLD GOOSEBERRY . . . . . . . . 151

22. DOUGHNUTS . . . . . . . . . 159

23. ABSENTEES . . . . . . . . . . 168

24. DUMMIES! . . . . . . . . . . 176

25. INTERLUDES . . . . . . . . . 185

26. EXPANSION . . . . . . . . . . 194

27. AXIOM . . . . . . . . . . . 202

28. SWEEPING ON . . . . . . . . . 209

29. ON YOUR BEAM . . . . . . . . 216

# *YOU*

## *Are the Adventure!*

## Chapter One

## EXPLORER'S ITCH

If you are in the habit of doing preliminary hops-skips-and-jumps through the unfamiliar books you pick up, to get their general flavor and direction, and to find out what happens on the last page, before settling down comfortably to move from word to word, I can save you time and effort by providing you with that information here at the beginning of this book.   It isn't, of course, the thing to do according to orthodox literary patterns, but who cares about that, so long as your way is eased in getting what you're looking for? Frankly and briefly, then, this book has to do with rocking chairs, thumbs, adventure, exploration, and You.   Yes, very much You!   As a matter of fact, from here on you become the leading character.

The book has a beginning, which of course is obvious, but unlike the ordinary run of books it has no ending.   When you reach the last page, you go straight through the back cover as though it weren't there.   That is, you do so, provided you have accumulated sufficient mental velocity, altitude, and visibility on the way through. And when you reach that point, you keep right on going throughout time, space, and even eternity itself. And that's traveling! Almost anything can happen to you around the bend of any of the following pages, but then please don't forget that almost anything can happen to me too; which of course is as it should be in all books having to do with adventure and exploration.

When I speak of adventuring and exploring, I do not mean that old-fashioned, dated, biological kind, with its geographical limitations, its standardized routines, its publicity posterings, and its ballyhoo. But adventuring and exploring that may be unlike anything you have experienced before on land, at sea, in the air, or even in your dreams. As a matter of fact, some of the things you will participate in, if you come along, are going to make the historical jump of that fabulous cow over the moon seem amateurish and commonplace. No fooling!

That's the kind of book you are in, my Hearty! And because it is so unconventional, it is only fair to warn you that from this point on you will have to move at your own intellectual, emotional, and philosophical risk. I cannot in any way be responsible for you. From here on, while we move out together, each of us is strictly on his own. So may I suggest, in view of all this, that you carefully examine your mental antenna to see if it is in fairly good working order, and that you loosen up and slack away on your thinking processes, so that there will be no static when moving away from the familiar.

It certainly would be interesting to know just how it came about that at this particular moment in the scheme of things your particular eyes should be zigzagging down the pages of this particular book. I know why I am in here between these two covers, but I wonder why you are! The reason, I suppose, could be almost anything between "a casual coincidence" and "predestination." One thing though is certain: you're not mousing around in here for nothing; you're looking for something! What that is is none of my business, of course. But if I were permitted a running broad guess, I'd say that you were more or less fed up with the ruts, routines, regulations, and restrictions of your biological everydayness. And that deep within you, where you do your private planning and plotting, there is a restless longing to escape, and to feel the tang and tingle of new horizons . . . new ideas . . . new relationships . . . and new experiences.

If this diagnosis should be correct, then, my

Hearty, you have what is technically known as Explorer's Itch! And Explorer's Itch, in case you are not familiar with it, is a peculiar visitation quite common to the human species. It is both capricious and disquieting, and affects people in as many varied ways as there are human beings. It is usually harmless, except with the undisciplined, and then it can be violent in the extreme. Explorer's Itch is an outward manifestation of an inner disturbance. It is caused by rebellion against one's own boundaries, boundaries he may have set for himself, or permitted others to set for him. It is mental, emotional, and spiritual mutiny against too much squeezed-inness. An invariable indication that the borders of one's being—seeing, knowing, and doing—need enlarging, and enriching.

I speak with a certain amount of authority in these matters, because Explorer's Itch has been doing things to me mentally and geographically for many years. If I may be frank and specific about it, it has exerted its pressure on me ever since a certain memorable morning once upon a time when, unwatched for a brief space by an overbusy mother, I wiggled out of freshly wrapped but loosely pinned diapers, ditto out of an ancient rocking cradle that should have been in a museum, and fell downstairs into the cellar, in what I still

[4]

maintain was a praiseworthy attempt to broaden my horizons, and to learn more about life at first hand.

Down through the intervening years, this itching incitement to wiggle out of whatever curtails my mental and physical freedom has been as much a part of me as my breathing. Indeed, in many ways they resemble one another. With breathing, the rhythm is inhale and exhale. With Explorer's Itch, it is income and outgo, income and ongo; in comes the incitement and out I go with it, blown out willy-nilly, as it were, in all sorts of directions, and on all sorts of quests. Often it merely sets me moving along picturesque, deserted roads or trails, fired with the desire to know where they go, and what they do when they get there. At other times the force of it sends me bouncing off to the most distant parts of the earth, merely to find out for myself what really goes on there and why.

What to do with Explorer's Itch when it takes possession of one's thinking and feelings is a problem of no mean proportions. It can sneak into one with the innocent gentleness of a soft, perfumed night breeze. Or it can do the reverse and come with dramatic suddenness, like an unexpected kick in the seat of one's pants, or, say, a depth bomb going off in the middle of one's emotions. But whatever way it comes, its effects are much the same—to fill one to overflowing with strange imaginings and notions, with even stranger flutterings and flusterings, and to cause him to "git up and git, from where he is t'wards where he ain't, but would like to be."

During my Rhode Island school days, when rules and regulations and the accompanying penalties were not to be taken lightly, Explorer's Itch and its expression was usually called "truancy," or "playing hooky." It indicated, according to the opinions then prevailing, that one having this mysterious inner longing for expansion and freedom was a shirker, an embryo escapist, a potential defective, and a specimen to be closely watched at all times. And not only that, but one who would most likely spend his oncoming years ducking down hypothetical byways, around hypothetical corners, and over hypothetical backfences, in order to escape having to do his duty as a one-hundred-per-cent American. I was doubly plagued in these philosophical and ethical matters by having inherited a granite-bound New England conscience, which, as the brilliant playwright Clyde Fitch once observed, permits one to do as he pleases, but prevents him from enjoying it.

In these swift-moving, kaleidoscopic days, however, when the starch is oozing out of so many traditions, conventions, beliefs, opinions, and ways of doing things, and when one can scarcely get set for the next incredible thing that happens, Explorer's Itch has not only taken on new significance, but even an air of respectability. It has been given various fancy, therapeutical, and poetical names, but of this you may be sure: whenever your thinking areas are suddenly flooded with straying thoughts, vagabond fancies, restless dissatisfaction, and the urge to wander and loiter, what you really have is plain, old-fashioned Explorer's Itch, caused by the friction of thinking and living in margins too narrow for you, and inciting you to get out of them and enlarge the borders of your being . . . your seeing . . . your knowing . . . and your doing.   Or else!

All the great experts in the lovely art of spacious and gracious living down through the ages had Explorer's Itch in chronic form.   Because of this, they were always seeking to escape from limiting local environments, if not physically, at least mentally and spiritually.   They were always in movement with their total selfhood.   Always heading outward and upward.   Always following their individual "inner lights."   Always adventuring. Always exploring.   Always attempting the impossible and usually accomplishing it.

To them man's unrest and desire for change was not to be frowned upon, but rather to be given good direction and encouraged. They regarded it as man's incessant hunger for the Infinite . . . his natural yearning for expansion . . . unfoldment . . . satisfaction . . . completeness . . . wholeness . . . unity . . . oneness . . . and perfection. They often spoke of it as "the stir of God in man." This divine Presence and Allness, they pointed out, is constantly revealing Itself to receptive minds and hearts. Is constantly forcing each of us, by one means or another, out of his little finite self and into his larger and real SELF, into his infinite, divine SELFHOOD.

Through their clear vision they were able to see that Life was, is, and always will be a constant process of moving on. Of continuous growth. Of never-ending expansion. As each one of us gives heed to these things, they said in their various ways, Life automatically becomes for him an exhilarating and profitable experience, not merely along the earth levels, but all the way from the human to the divine . . . from the finite to the infinite . . . from the mortal to the immortal . . . and from the terrestrial to the celestial.

*Chapter Two*

## THE ANCIENT GESTURE

If it wouldn't startle you too much and make you drop this book like a hot potato, do you know what I'd like to do?  Dwarf this human body of mine to the right size for such an undertaking, whisk it through space the way elfin folk travel, and straddle it atop one of these pages you are looking at.  Then from the friendliest depths in me I'd like to shout a neighborly "Hello!" across to you.  And I would like to do this not as an Author, spelled with a capital "A," anxious to talk down his carefully powdered literary nose, at what he hopes is a sympathetic, admiring, and cash-paying reader, spelled with a small "r," but rather as one oft-puzzled but adventurous earth-rider, giving the sign of recognition to a fellow-adventurer.

Then if you had the time and inclination for it, I'd like to drop all formalities between us and, mentally naked and unashamed, swap ideas and experiences with you about the world in general and you and me in particular.  Think how in-

[9]

teresting it would be, for instance, if you and I dared really to open up and exchange our innermost thoughts about everything we cared to talk about, without fear of repercussions in the form of mental criticism or subsequent gossip! There are things I have inwardly acquired while exploring Life that you might find helpful, but there is much that you think about and have experienced that would, I know, be most beneficial to me, if you felt free to unwrap yourself and really let go.

One of the things I should particularly like to know about you is how you manage to keep yourself economically and socially afloat in these days of strife, strain, and contrariety. What charts or other navigation aids do you use, for instance, to steer yourself through the bewilderments and snags of the world we live in? And especially, just what do you do when you have the urge to see and experience more of life, but are blocked in on every side by "circumstances?" Do you, I wonder, capitulate easily to things of this sort? And having done so, do you let others do your adventuring and exploring for you, through the medium of books, magazines, the radio, the theatre, and motion pictures? Or have you a special skill for wiggling out of the limiting routines of conventional existence, and maintaining your freedom? I wonder!

[10]

If you'll brace yourself for the shock, I'll tell you what I do when Old Man Circumstance springs one of his temporary traps around my plans and activities. I park my body in a rocking chair, set them both to oscillating in my favorite rhythm, and then, using one of my preaxial digits as a reminder and compass, thumb my way out into all sorts of exciting and profitable adventures. Sounds rather balmy, doesn't it? As though I might also go in for dancing around mulberry bushes with the pixies, whenever the moon is in the right ascendancy and the fairy queen has given her royal permission! But it isn't nearly so irrational as it appears. And it isn't mere whimsy, either! Or a new method for indulging in daydreaming. Or a personal idiosyncrasy, skidding and out of control. It is, you can quite easily discover for yourself, realism of the first magnitude. Realism with a new bonnet on its head, stepping out and going places. Realism that surpasses even imagination.

I will have to admit, though, that thumbing one's way out on exploring expeditions while seat-to-seat with a rocking chair is not conventional procedure. Indeed, one must have a mind and a heart for the unusual even to contemplate such goings-on. Were defense needed for them, I would simply go to my files and trundle out stacks

[11]

of documentary evidence to prove, among other things: (1) that most human beings become bewildered, balk, and bolt, whenever they come face-to-face with a new idea, (2) that almost every non-conformist, in every field of endeavor since time began, was regarded as more or less mentally unsound and a potentially dangerous fellow, until the slow-moving mass mind, ever fearful of change, was able to catch up with him, and (3) that virtually every expedition that ever set out to attempt anything original was someone's "folly" that was moving "contrary to reason and common sense." At least, it was until the explorer returned with fresh knowledge to share with his doubting and unimaginative fellow beings. So you see, when I thumb out from my rocking chair, I do so in the wake of a gloriously mad but at the same time an achieving assortment of Originals.

In the modern style of hitchhiking, where the thumb plays such an important part, one's progress depends upon the favorable consideration of others. In thumbing out from a rocking chair one has to depend entirely on himself. And while the rocking chair is a great aid in ventures of this sort, it is not absolutely essential. For if one knows how to go about it, he can take off from wherever he happens to be, provided the surrounding atmosphere is clear of the distracting noises made by human beings, in their efforts to convince themselves and others that they are alive. The pivot point in these expeditions is always the thumb, or to be more technically correct, the thumbprint.

The use of the thumb as an aid in moving one's physicality from one geographical spot to another is of very ancient lineage, much more so than one would ordinarily believe. Down through the ages men have stood along roadsides in most countries making the familiar thumb gesture, and by means of this sign language asking, or demanding, to be picked up and helped along in their respective journeys. How far back into the past the gesture goes, no one could possibly say. But to one fact I can attest: down in fascinating underground tombs of once-famous rulers, in the Valley of the Kings, in Egypt, I have seen vividly colored, historical picture-writings that plainly illustrated the fact that the men of those early dynasties were experts in using their thumbs to promote rides in chariots or with camel-trains. Those ancient Egyptians may have lacked the proficiency and variety of rides available at the present time, but that didn't prevent them from developing thumb-swinging into an art rarely seen from the seat of an automobile today.

Here in these United States thumbing rides has

become such an interwoven part of the texture of travel that it has developed a ritualistic form of its own. On almost any highway from border to border, and from coast to coast, you will find members of this large, unorganized fraternity, expectantly waiting for you to come along and move them nearer to wherever it is they are planning to go. If you will observe closely, you will discover that each one of them is using the identical stance of head, body, arms, and legs as did all the others. That he has the same general air about him, the same set expression. That he is making almost exactly the same degree of arc when he swings his thumb. And that if you pass him by, he flings in your direction the same "this-to-you!" as did all the others.

It is astonishing how far some of these roadside adventurers have been able to thumb their way, without having to spend money for transportation. I have come upon them in all sorts of out-of-the-way corners of the world, even in such seemingly-impossible-to-reach places as unfrequented islands in the Dutch East Indies. Some of them had even thumbed their way completely around the earth, both Easterly and Westerly, which as everyone knows who has done much traveling, is a top-notch performance at any time. The tales some of these wanderers have shared with me

[14]

of their thumbings and bummings are among my most treasured memories.

What particularly interested me about these colorful vagabonds was their zeal for adventurous living, their audacity, their enterprise, their sense of fun, their adaptability, their courage in living their own lives as they wanted to live them. Like those natural philosophers and adventurers—dogs and children—they met each day with eager curiosity, wonder, and high expectation. Like children and dogs, they took life just as it came along, without regret or complaint, and made it yield them rich dividends in happiness and satisfaction. They neither worried about the past nor speculated about the future, being far too busily engaged in the here and the now of things. For them, like the children and the dogs, every turn in the road was a fresh world to be explored and enjoyed, and everything met held the prospect of an exhilarating experience.

But while the thumbing-out exploits of these rare adventurers were truly amazing, they are as nothing to the adventures I usually stir up with the help of my thumb and a rocking chair. Those fellows merely thumbed their way around the earth. I not only do that, but I thumb my way completely off the earth. I go over the edge of it and leave it behind me for just what the astron-

omers say it is, "a fleck of dust in immensity." I
flick off the fleck and get out into immensity. I
go out where there is no earth to stand on, no sky
over one's head, no horizons at all. Out where
definitions and limitations evaporate. Out where
one can unplug his capacities for perceiving, receiving, containing, and utilizing. Out where one
can spread himself to something like his true proportions, and live as an illimitable being among
illimitable things.

*Chapter Three*

## THUMBS UP!

If you are what many of the more critical commentators of the human scene are fond of classifying and tagging as "an average citizen," which can mean almost anything, but which usually specifically implies that you don't go in very extensively for doing your own thinking, and so are easy to mass and manipulate, it is probable that you pay relatively little attention to those thumbs of yours. Except, perhaps, as you crack down on one of them with a hammer, have the nails manicured, use them to slide playing cards along, moisten to turn the page of a book, or lay against your nose in moments of jest or irritation.

In view of this possibility, I want to pause here long enough in our journey toward the back cover to introduce, or at least to reintroduce, you to your thumbs. If you don't know them very well, this should be a memorable occasion for you. It could turn out to be the greatest turning point in your life to date. For in "tremendous trifles" no greater than this, Life often spins around, opens up, and reveals to us its richest treasures. But even if none of this should happen to you, your remeeting with your thumbs this way will enable you to understand more realistically why that stirring call and gesture—"THUMBS UP!"—borrowed from ancient Roman times when the people in the Colosseum, by pointing their thumbs up or down, had the power of life or death over the contestants, has come into such popular use today among those who are trying to maintain freedom for the individual.

As your part in this reunion, may I suggest that you get a magnifying glass, aim it at the bulb of one of your thumbs, and have a searching look at that small but highly important part of your anatomy. Your first impression may be one of "just thumb," with many tiny, meaningless lines squiggling in various directions. But there is lots more sense to it than that. If you will observe closely, you will see that each of those lines is perfectly etched into your skin. Each of those lines is there for a definite purpose as far as you are concerned. Each line has a technical name, known to experts in human identification in all parts of the world. The lines are known as ridges, the spaces in between them, furrows; and their various characteristics are classified and reclassified under such headings as loops, whorls, accidentals, composites, deltas, and so forth. Those various lines form a perfect and complete pattern. Your particular pattern was on your thumb the day you were born. It will remain there just as you see it as long as you have that thumb. Thumbprints and finger-prints never change between birth and death, ex-cept as the lines increase in size and proportion with the other parts of the body. That thumb-print of yours is exclusively your own design. There is not another like it anywhere. There never has been. There never will be. That print on the face of your thumb is the indication . . . the mark . . . the sign . . . the symbol . . . and the proof, of your everlasting identity as an indi-vidual. May I repeat the last part of that? The proof of your everlasting identity as an individual!

Throughout the world today there are unguess-able billions upon billions of still more billions upon billions of thumbprints. Before these ap-peared there were centuries upon centuries of still more billions upon billions of thumbprints. Yet in all this thought-staggering assortment of white, brown, yellow, and black thumbprints, there has not been one single print like yours. Think that one over for awhile! The search for duplicate thumbprints has been going on ever since the early centuries, when the Chinese, with their customary wisdom, began using them for sealing

[19]

documents, signing contracts, and proving identity. It has continued without interruption down to the present day, when government bureaus throughout the world exchange vast numbers of prints daily, in their work of identifying and searching for people.

And yet with all this search and research, all this checking and rechecking, all this analysis and study, the wonder still remains, that no one has ever been able to find two thumbprints alike. Amazing! Well, yes, and then again, no! Depending on how you look at it. "Yes!" when you come face to face with the facts for the first time. But "No!" when you take into consideration the equally astonishing fact that no one has ever been able to find two blades of grass alike, or two leaves, or two snowflake crystals, or two grains of sand, or two anythings.

That's the kind of a universe you are in, my Hearty! Magnificent individuality here, there, and everywhere. But, and this is even more important to observe, magnificent individuality and variety in equally magnificent unity and oneness. Each of us a distinguishable and distinguished note, so to speak, in The Great Eternal Theme Song of Creation. This proof of your individuality, of your distinctness, and of your uniqueness, should cheer you immeasurably. And it should give to your life all sorts of interesting extensions, unless, by chance, the police happen to be stalking you with a set of your thumbprints and finger-prints. I sincerely hope this isn't true, of course, but if it should be, take my tip as a former crime reporter, and turn yourself in at the nearest police station. For sooner or later, no matter how clever you believe yourself to be, you will unintentionally leave the mark of your identity on something or other for trained eyes and minds to detect, and the police car will be around to collect you.

You might be able to elude the police, of course. It has been done before and will be many times again. But always remember this: The percen-tages are always working against you. If you were a novice in matters of this kind, you might have the quaint notion that you could outsmart the police by altering your thumbprints and finger-prints with sandpaper, acid, a razor blade, or even a professional surgical operation. But in the end, as you looked out through prison bars, you would find that all you had brought through the experi-ence was the quaint notion, and an assortment of painful memories and flesh. Even if you took a red-hot poker, as many have, and blistered the bulbs of your thumbs and fingers, and watched the prints completely disappear with the dead cuticle, you would find, when the new skin grew again, as

[21]

new skin has a way of doing, that the very same prints were back again without one tiny line missing, or one tiny line being out of place.

If you fancied the extreme in matters of this kind, you could, of course, cut off your thumbs and fingers. That certainly would put a very definite end to the telltale prints. And how! But it wouldn't baffle the police, not in the least. They would simply begin checking your identity by the prints on the bottom of your feet. If you cut off your feet, they would look for your identity on your ears. And if you cut off your ears, they would move with the same methodical exactness to other parts of your body, until you learned—that is, if there were anything left of you by that time —how utterly impossible it is for you to escape being you.

In other words, you are a Somebody. You cannot get away, now or ever, from this great fact about you. No matter what the number and the variety of your failures . . . or your present shortcomings . . . or the things you seem to lack . . . or how low down in the scale of human values others may rate you, or you may rate yourself . . . the truth about you at every moment of the day and night is that in your real being you are a Somebody. Not a Somebody on special occasions when you may have the temporary admiration and applause of others, but a Somebody all the time. A Somebody without an equal, now or ever. Every bit of the seen and the unseen "you" proclaims this, whether you are aware of it or not. Proclaims continuously that you are a highly valuable, self-contained, and complete Identity. Proclaims you to be an indispensable living Fact among other equally indispensable living Facts. No greater distinction will ever be conferred upon you.

Through this highly individualized Being of yours, which extends illimitably beyond your physical-material-human frontiers, you automatically become an expression and interpreter of the great creative Intelligence pervading all things. And your functioning is through whatever message, talent, gift, grace, or service comes naturally to you, and is a blessing to your fellow-beings. No matter how you have been regarding the situation, the fact about you is that you always have been, are now, and always will be, your individual self in the infinite and eternal Plan ... Purpose ... Harmony ... and Rhythm. Without you in your place, doing your job in your way, the universe would not and could not be the perfectly functioning Arrangement it is. Perfectly functioning, it should be added, in spite of all the humanly generated beliefs to the contrary.

But you don't have to take my word for it. You

can find all the clues you will need, and all the proofs too, on the bulbs of those thumbs and fingers of yours.   That is why they are there.   To remind you again and again that you are you. Not someone else.  Or like anyone else.  Or even resembling anyone else.  Ten priceless thumb- and fingerprints, telling you in their silent but eloquent way that you are not restricted to a family, a group, a nation, or even to the earth itself, but belong to a spiritually mental process of infinite proportions.  Ten priceless fingerprints, warning you that you have an important place to fill in the scheme of life, and to be up and doing something about it.  Ten priceless fingerprints, ever urging you to come out of your restricted, regulated conformity, and take the position and attitude rightly belonging to you.   Ten priceless fingerprints, challenging you moment by moment to be your real self in everything you think, say, and do.  And to defend this glorious heritage to the utmost, come what may.

## Chapter Four

## HELL-DIVERS

"That's all very well to be setting down on paper as a theory in the quiet of your library, or wherever it is that you write this stuff," I shall imagine you thinking to yourself as you come out of that last chapter, perhaps a bit suspicious of what I may be up to, and rightly so; "but the important thing is how can anyone make things like that work in a practical world like the one we are living in? How, for instance, would anyone use such theories when he started out in the morning to try to earn a living for himself and a family? Or how could anyone maintain his individuality intact, sweet-smelling and contributive, and at the same time steer himself successfully and ethically through a world so given over to rowdydowdy mass thinking, mass emotions, mass action, and mass misbehavior?"

I haven't any pat answers for these questions, even though I made them up, nor have I any personal panaceas wrapped and ready for delivery. It cannot be done that easily. For, as you undoubtedly know, if we set aside for the moment such basic problems as food, sex, the vanity urges, and the preservation of life, there is no more intricate difficulty confronting the members of the human species today than that of how most effectively to restore individuality, in its fullest and finest sense, to every man, woman, and child on earth.    That is, how to keep their individualities functioning as their own individualities rather than as copies of someone else's.    If you have tried to do this with your own individuality in your contacts with others, and particularly in your social, business, political, and religious affiliations, you know how difficult it is to do in even a middling sort of way.

The fainthearted among us, those who habitually anchor their lives as close inshore as possible in order to avoid wind, weather, and experience, believe such maintenance of individuality to be not only a waste of effort but impossible, especially if one has any ambition to get along favorably and comfortably with his fellow beings.    Their belief is that when one insists upon being "different," by moving out mentally and otherwise on his own instead of keeping in strict conformity with the others, he not only stirs them up unnecessarily but precipitates himself into all sorts of opposition, misunderstandings, and conflict.    All of which is avoidable, they point out, by keeping one's mental and physical head on a level with the dominant people and moving in precise step with them, whatever the direction.

At least that was the quite general attitude until comparatively recently, when that series of super-violent international explosions took place, and our supposedly reliable physical, material, and human props began letting us down with thuds, squawks, and groanings never before equaled in all history. Without the slightest regard for wealth, fame, family, or influence, we were all flung abruptly out of one kind of a world into another. Flung into a world so different, so swift-changing, and so bewildering, that virtually everyone found himself dazed, a bit scared, and forced at least to try to do his own thinking on a swim-or-sink basis.

Almost overnight each of us became in some degree a mental and spiritual explorer, not from choice but because we had to. The pressure of the world-wide cataclysm was too heavy, too personal, and the events going on all about us too lurid and terrifying. Our petty little worlds of self-interest were turned upside down, inside out, and kicked about in the most disrespectful way. We began reaping the whirlwinds of our individual and collective sowings, and we didn't like

[27]

them. Then, as you will recall, if you watch such trends, began one of the greatest stampedes in all history. It wasn't a biological and geographical stampede but a mental and spiritual one. It was an individual scramble to find something or SOMETHING upon which one could really depend in such stormy times.

Apparently the only ones who knew how to ride the world-wide gales victoriously were those spiritually minded adventurers and explorers who had conditioned themselves for just such happenings. And they—bless them for their sparkling examples!—recognizing the great need for the national and international cleansing of minds and hearts, bitter and afflictive though it seemed to be, took to the disturbed conditions about them the way those vivacious, fearless, little hell-divers of the duck family take to tumbling seas and a heavy surf. Indeed, it would be difficult to say whether these particular humans or the hell-divers get the greater satisfaction out of their common specialty of meeting whatever comes their way with relish and enthusiasm; of riding over and through difficulties, rather than permitting the difficulties to ride over or through them.

This seems to have been true of human beings of this type and of hell-divers ever since they started functioning, both of them having an overabundance of "what it takes." Somewhere in their evolvements both types learned the neat trick of fixing a calm eye on life, regardless of how it happened to present itself, and then flinging themselves into it with everything they had that was flingable. Watch either of them in action and you will note that the basis of their technique is not to struggle with Life, but rather to blend themselves with It and move in Its full rhythm. And Life, it would appear, respects them for this, makes way for them, and takes care of them, whatever the surface disturbance.

Unfortunately for us humans, the hell-divers have no historians among them capable of recording in any of our mediums of expression their philosophical and ethical attitudes toward everyday existence. Or to convey to us, so that the average citizen might understand, how it is possible for them to keep their relations so simple, serene, and satisfying, in a world so boisterously antisocial. But you can read about their semblances in human form—those stouthearted, trouble-defying mental explorers who had the courage and ability to follow their own inner light and to move out into the unknown in search of new facets of truth, beauty, and goodness to share with the rest of us.

I have great admiration for adventurers of this

kind. I like to read about them, but better still to talk with them in that intimacy of understanding wherein thoughts are unselfed and heart attuned to heart. I am privileged to know many of them in almost all parts of the world. Considering the differences in their national, educational, religious, social, philosophical, and economic backgrounds, they would seem to be as unrelated as human beings possibly could be. And yet their understanding of universal Life and relations is so comprehensive and so all-inclusive that all of them could swap fundamentals, purposes, attitudes, and practices, and then move along their respective ways, without losing a beat or creating the slightest disharmony in the lovely rhythm of their daily lives. Which, I am sure you will agree with me, is touching Oneness in a big way.

If you could tiptoe mentally near any of these truly great adventurers, you would be able to pick up valuable tips on how to make ordinary, everyday existence more interesting and productive. For one thing, you would probably be most impressed by the emphasis each of them places on individuality, on being thoroughly himself in everything he thinks, says, and does, but at the same time expecting you to do the same thing too. They are individualists of the first magnitude, undimable stars to set one's course by. Individuality to them is never personality-strutting, or detached self-centeredness, or any form of isolation. It is their recognition of their part, responsibility, and opportunity in the universal plan, and they are constantly doing something about it. They keep ever active the ancient law to glorify God and live the Golden Rule, inwardly as well as outwardly. And thus each of them takes the world as he finds it, and in his own individual way tries to make it better and lovelier for others as he goes along his earth-journey.

One phase of their livingness is especially worth noting. They first reduce the universe to their spiritually minded selves, and then through consecrated and unselfed effort expand their spiritually minded selves to include the Universe. Nothing throughout the length and breadth, or the height and depth, of life is outside the range of their interest and affections. Their loyalties are universal. They see and experience celestial things while riding the earth like the rest of us, but then they have something carefully cultivated within them that makes it possible for them to see and experience celestial things. They exemplify in the most brilliant and practical way possible the age-old command to FIND THYSELF . . . KNOW THYSELF . . . BE THYSELF . . . and SHARE THYSELF.

*Chapter Five*

## ADVENTURERS

One of my proudest possessions is my collection of adventuring friends, which I have been carefully hand-picking up and down the world's highways, and in and out of its byways, for many years. It's a rare assortment of originals, if I do say so myself, made up of men and women of many nationalities, with all sorts of backgrounds as well as all sorts of unrelated interests. If they could all be brought together in one place at the same time, looked at and listened to, it certainly would make front-page newspaper copy. Each of them is a pre-eminent individualist. Each of them is distinct in his particular field. Each of them a deviate in the better meaning of that term. And each of them a past master in the art of hanging on to his identity and freedom in a world so given over to regimentation.

The collection includes famed explorers of deserts, jungles, and arctic regions; soldiers of fortune more colorful than any book that could be written about them; mountain-climbers; gentle-speaking metaphysicians able to prove man's dominion over material conditions; plain and fancy vagabonds who are apt to turn up anywhere at any time; self-effacing mystics in out-of-the-way parts of the world, surrounded by silence and humbly listening to the Voice beyond all silence; nomads who exchange ideas with animals, birds, insects, snakes, and "things" more intelligently than man ordinarily does with man; modern-day saints living their goodness instead of talking about it; beachcombers, lone ocean navigators, poets, teachers, philosophers, artists, musicians, inventors, nonsqueaking religionists, and a long list of "nobodies" with great inner wealth, which they share as birds do their song and flowers their perfume.

One of my particular favorites in the collection is a specimen I found in Shanghai, China. That I should happen to cross his trail there is in itself significant, for previous to the Second World War Shanghai was rated by the knowing ones as the greatest adventure-providing city in the world. It was an adventurer's paradise, a bizarre, alluring, and incredible place at any hour of the day or night. Anything could happen there, and usually did. One never had to hunt for adventure in Shanghai. Step in any direction from wherever you happened to be in the city and you were in it. Stand still and the adventure came looking for you.

I shall always be grateful that I first met Shanghai, socially and otherwise, in company with one of the greatest of adventurers, the debonair, scintillating, gay, athletic, unpredictable Douglas Fairbanks, Senior. Fairbanks, with his unbounded imagination, his vitality, his pranks, his boyish curiosity, his enthusiasm, his ambition to be the first to leap-frog over the moon, and his great talent for turning himself into a hero of screen adventure for those who were either unable or too lazy to provide it for themselves. "The great high priest of make-believe!" someone once called him. He was that and more. He belonged to the unclassables, the indefinables.

The Fairbanks and I were gypsy-footing it around the world in the grand manner, or perhaps it would be more correct to say that he was doing the gypsy-footing and I was trying to keep up with him. It was the "life of Riley" on a golden-fleeced cloud. He was as free and as variable as the wind, and as delightfully irresponsible too, but that irresponsibility usually provided our most thrilling and unusual experiences. Our heaviest problem in Shanghai was trying to decide what to do when, and if, we left Shanghai. There were tentative plans for an expedition into the Gobi Desert to capture some long-haired tigers and fetch them back to Hollywood. There was talk of a hunting expedition into Indo-China, a flying trip into remote parts of Russia, a visit to Tibet, and a wild but alluring scheme for prowling around with a bandit band in the back country of China.

In the midst of this indecision, a reception was staged for The Fairbanks in one of the large hotels on the Bund. It was an extraordinary affair even for Shanghai, for milling about at the party was a crowd composed of almost every known type of professional and amateur chance-taker, men who lived solely for thrills and specialized in dangerous enterprises. I happened to be talking to one of them across a plate of most excellent Chinese food. He was internationally known as an explorer, had been almost everywhere, and was an authority on Oriental jungles. Hoping to pick up information for The Fairbanks, I asked him where he thought one should go to find the best adventure, expecting quite naturally that he would tell me about the jungles with which he was so well acquainted.

For some seconds he eyed me appraisingly, as though trying to figure out along what mental levels I moved. Then he said: "My personal preference is for sitting in a rocking chair, and exploring the undiscovered regions in my own mind."

[35]

Nothing could have startled me more, especially in such a place and at such a party. Then, before the breath was really back in me, he went on: "We explorers have conquered practically all the geographical frontiers but not the mental ones. We know almost nothing about the oceans and continents lying still undiscovered in the hinterlands of our own minds. That is the real challenge of the future. Geographical exploration is comparatively simple. Mental exploration is more difficult. It takes more initiative, more daring, and more courage, but the returns in accomplishment and satisfaction are much greater."

As soon as I could get adjusted to the surprise of it all, I knew what he was talking about, for I had found this same viewpoint, although in widely varying degrees, in virtually all the more experienced explorers I knew. Reduced to its essence, their collective conviction was this: that though one explore every spot on earth, fly as high in the stratosphere as machinery and oxygen will lift him, or burrow deeper underground than anyone has ever been before, in the end he can arrive at but one conclusion. This! That the greatest wonder to be found anywhere is one's own self . . . his mind . . . his consciousness . . . his subjective state of being . . . his thinking areas

. . . his world of awareness . . . that which makes him so uniquely what he is.

That I could understand, and understanding it knew why he liked to explore his own mind. But what puzzled me was how the rocking chair fitted into such ventures. He was most obliging when I asked. "To understand why I like to use a rocking chair," he said, "it is necessary to remember that everything is in a state of continuous motion, or vibration, or rhythm, or call it what you will. Instead of doing this, however, and recognizing that we have to move with this great Cosmic force whether we like it or not, most of us try to disregard it. We feel that we are independent and unrelated items in the universe, privileged to do what we please, as we please, regardless of anyone or anything except ourselves. That is what causes all our trouble and grief. I use a rocking chair to help counteract this. I use it to rock myself into physical and mental rhythm with the Universe. The Orientals know how helpful rocking back and forth can be in efforts of this kind, only they rock on their heels or from a cross-legged position."

His method, he went on to explain, was to rock slowly backward and forward, keeping his thinking moving outward and as much away from himself as possible, until the picture of himself as a human being grew dim or faded out completely, and he became just his thinking, capable of moving in any direction, and without restrictions of any kind.   He spoke of it as hunting for new countries or states of mind in the vast, unseen Universe lying still undiscovered all about us, or rather, he added, within us.

He predicted that we would all have to become mental explorers sooner or later, because of the way the scientists were causing the material universe to disappear before our very eyes.   "They are insisting with ever-increasing proof," he said, "that the universe of mechanized matter is not external to us at all, but inside us—that is, inside each individual mind—and that it is made of the same substance as mental ideas.   Which means that everything contrary to a spiritually mental universe is as temporary and as fleeting as vapor."

At which point I moved him into a front position in my collection of adventurers and explorers.

*Chapter Six*

## SUPERVAGABOND

Thus was I intrigued into becoming a rocking-chair adventurer and explorer. To the uninitiated this could sound like looking for the perfect way in which to dawdle, day-dream, and do nothing—that is, nothing beyond the effort required to formulate opinions as to what ought to be done with the rest of the universe to make it mesh better with our private views. Like for instance those "rocking-chair admirals," with a minimum of practical experience, who used to sit on yacht-club porches on pleasant days and hand down "Supreme Court decisions" on how every boat in the harbor should have been sailed. Real rocking-chair adventuring and exploring, however, is something incomparably different, as all will enthusiastically agree who have ever ventured out in this way, into what my Shanghai friend would have called "their real essence."

On my first experimental rocking-chair exploit, after that episode in China, I began making all sorts of what to me were thrillingly new discoveries about the universe in general and myself in particular. The method was elemental in its simplicity. I found a chair with a good roll to it, took it out into a quiet garden, placed my body in it, started chair and body rolling at a very slow tempo, took the padlocks off my thoughts and let them go where they pleased. Every time I did this, I gradually became aware that what seemed to be a more mental and more expanded me was moving along in a rhythm and harmony almost baffling description. The spiral of it went like this: the more I thought, the more I explored; the more I explored, the more I expanded; the more I expanded, the more new values I found; the more new values I found, the more I was enriched; and the more I was enriched, the more abundantly I lived. It never failed to work just like that. And that upswinging spiral with its corresponding rewards would continue, I knew, as long as I continued to be my part in it to the best of my ability.

But that was by no means all, for the more I wandered about in the back country of my own mind observing all I could, the clearer it became that I did not have to make great objective and physical efforts in order to find adventure, nor was it necessary for me to limit my explorations to the geographical any more. For, and this was the breath-taking part of it all, I MYSELF WAS THE

ADVENTURE! I contained it! I included it! The more I thought about it, the more obvious it became. To know or to experience anything at all, I had to be aware of it, I reasoned to myself; and the only place in which I can be aware of anything, from the smallest thing I can identify to the universe itself, is within the borders of my own mind, or consciousness; within this astonishing but so little-known mental embodiment that I call "ME." "How can I possibly know anything outside my own thinking?" I asked of the atmosphere about me. And something in the atmosphere flung back, "You can't!" And that, of course, settled that.

The Fairbanks, to hop back to him again by way of illustrating a rather interesting point, was a most unusual adventurer as everyone knows who ever saw any of his motion pictures or read of his exploits. He WAS a most unusual adventurer, did I say? Pardon me, he still is a most unusual adventurer, for nothing could possibly impair or end the particular assortment of mental qualities he had; those mental qualities that made him what he so uniquely was, and still is. It is because of this unusual combination of inner qualities in him, qualities that gave him such conspicuous distinction, vitality, and originality in being and expression, that The Fairbanks has long been one of the

[41]

highly favored specimens in my collection of rare adventurers and explorers.

Following that reception in Shanghai, The Fairbanks and I moved around the rest of the world as only he knew how to manage such things. There was no itinerary, no plan, and often what seemed like no sense to it at all. It was the nearest to bird irresponsibility and bird flight I have ever experienced, and not greatly unlike the technique of that famous goofy bird that always flew backward because he was more interested in where he had been than in where he was going. The only thing that ever slowed us down was eating and sleeping and waiting for him to write autographs for film fans. That out of the way, we were always off again, just where never being quite clear until we arrived somewhere-or-other, and he decided that was the place.

Moving about with him in this supervagabondish way, listening to him inwardly tick, and watching him react to all sorts of things outwardly, was like being in the middle of a modernized fairy story, delightful but unpredictable. Traveling with him, as all his close friends found out sooner or later, required at least some actively working remnant of one's child-heart, a rimless imagination, flexibility, swift adaptability, a broad sense of fun, a fondness for the unusual in adventure, a

[42]

talent for being conventional and unconventional at the same time, and "bent knees" for jumpability. Thus equipped, one could synchronize with him fairly well, and so be ready, as was always necessary, to leap either mentally or physically without warning in any given direction or in no direction at all.

While I had all sorts of adventures with The Fairbanks, the most exciting and interesting, odd as it may seem, were neither geographical, social, nor, strictly speaking, even human. They were off the earth entirely. They were mental and spiritual. But please note that when the term spiritual is used, it does not refer to religion in any of its organized forms and ceremonies, but to religion as an individual way of life with an upward and outward swing to it; to religion as an individual adventure in search of more of what is enduringly beautiful, good, and true.

These adventures usually took place on the top deck of some ship during sun-tanning hours, the rolling motion of the ship being a most satisfying substitute for the rhythm of a rocking chair. During these occasions we would spread our bodies on favored deck spots side by side, leave them for the sun to work on, and then, as mental-beings, or ideas, unencumbered by physicality or limitations of any sort, zoom out together but individually

[43]

into what the poet Wordsworth was fond of calling "the mind's eternal Heaven." We always got out into thought areas where one's opportunities for exploring, discovering, and enjoying were bounded only by his ability to think and his capacity to receive and to contain. We usually swapped findings at the turning of the bodies, or when we had to take them to lower decks in order to be human beings again. The distances to which that Fairbanks could imagine himself, and the things he could find out there, many of which he used in his pictures, would have made that famous fabulist Aesop green with envy.

Through the medium of the stage and screen millions of people scattered all over the world became well acquainted with the producing and acting Doug Fairbanks, with the athletic Doug, the social Doug, the globe-trotting Doug, and the Doug who with such little effort made such enlivening newspaper and magazine copy. But relatively few, even among his friends, ever got to know the real Doug, that Doug who, while riding the earth temporarily disguised as a human being, was really living in a magic universe of his own, which he carried around with him, so to speak, like children do, and poets, and sages, and saints, and other divinely wise "irresponsibles," who do

[44]

not permit their inner eye to grow dim, or their. hearts to become cold and soggy.

Unimaginative people with dull perception, and probably fallen arches too, had difficulty in either seeing into, or even understanding, that inner kingdom of his, except perhaps when now and then they caught some faint glimpse of it in one of his films and felt better for the experience. Indeed, he didn't quite understand it himself much of the time, which often caused him to assume various kinds of outward pretendings in order to cover up his confusion. That inner kingdom was the only place in which one could find the real Douglas Fairbanks. In there was the starting point for that sparkling new era in the world of entertainment that he inaugurated, an era that veritably ended when he made his last picture.

*Chapter Seven*

## RHYTHM

If you were fortunate enough to have ridden in one of those old-fashioned, automatic rocking cradles when you were a baby. And if a few years later you knew the thrill of arming yourself with a wooden sword, climbing into the saddle of a high-spirited, gaily painted rocking horse, and galloping all over the kingdom of your imagination on all sorts of hazardous enterprises. Then it isn't going to be the least difficult for you to understand why a rocking chair can be so important in helping one open up new regions for exploration and adventure, even though one may regard himself as too grown up and too far beyond such things. Indeed, the knowledge gained in the transition from rocking cradle to rocking horse, and from rocking horse to rocking chair, is almost indispensable if one would get the pure essence of real adventure into the fiber of his being.

Taking for granted that you were well rocked as a baby, either in a cradle or in the arms of one who had a genuine feeling for melody and swing, it is then reasonable to assume that the first impression to dawn over the horizon of your world of awareness was one of most agreeable motion. Of being in rhythmical relation with everything about you. As though you were dancing with all Creation and all Creation dancing with you, even though, to the eyes aimed in your direction, you may have seemed to be merely a helpless, rather stupid, but awfully cute little dumpling-darling making meaningless gestures with your arms and legs and still more meaningless sounds in your throat.

Paradoxical as it may seem, the truth of the matter is that you actually were dancing with all Creation, and all Creation dancing with you. As a matter of fact, it would have been impossible for you to have avoided taking part in that Cosmic merriment. Unconsciously and involuntarily you were being your part in the harmony and rhythm of all existence. You were "doing your stuff" in the great, eternal Dance of Life. It was a happy, carefree life for you then, and it should be even more so for you now as part of your divine heritage; unless, by chance, your contacts with the world have darkened your vision, soured you, and thus thrown you out of step with the universal rhythm. But you hadn't been educated away from it then. You hadn't lost the sound of the clear beat of it. You were moving with it! Rock-

ing with it! Dancing with it! In all the glow
and glory of your fragrant, scintillating, unspoiled
young selfhood!

Had you been able at that time to have broken
away from those handicapping limitations that
practically all grownups fasten on children, you
could have stirred up some whopping adventures
in those rock-a-bye-baby days of yours, right under
the noses of your lynx-eyed guardians, and without their knowing anything about it, too. Suppose, for instance—and first-class supposing is an
important part of the equipment of every mental
adventurer—that, instead of having to go through
the long, involved, difficult process of growing up
and getting educated, a magic something happened in your baby mind, like light suddenly being switched on in a dark room, and you found
yourself fully educated.

There's a situation for you! The physical part
of you is lying apparently helpless, in whatever it
is they keep you in, while the mental part of you,
with perfect knowledge and awareness, is moving
all over the place, without those keepers of yours
knowing anything about it. By the magic wand
of make-believe, you have been set free not only
from conventional baby restrictions, but from all
grown-up ones as well. Which means that you
have an abundance of wisdom, that you can reason

[48]

analytically and correctly, and so are able to distinguish between truth and error, and between facts and counterfacts, no matter what appearance they assume. Moreover, you have a keen awareness of what great thinkers have been trying to make plain to mankind for centuries, namely, that one's mentality is not inside his physical body, but, on the contrary, that his physical body is a concept inside his mentality.

Purely for the fun of the thing, and by way of giving your imagination a workout, let's whirl you back to those baby days of yours and tilt you into some new kind of make-believe adventure. Remember that, while your physical body is baby-size and confined to a crib or cradle, your thinking is capable of moving around in boundless orbits. You would, of course, have to take off on this adventure mentally, and taking off mentally you would travel mentally, like all the top-flight adventurers in this and every other age. You would range, not as a human being with an idea, or an assortment of them, but entirely as an idea, an idea without the least need for anything human or material. Being an idea, you would, of course, move with all the lightness, indestructibility, speed, and freedom of an idea. And nothing could slow you down or stop you except you yourself.

It is quite likely that the first thing to arrest

your attention in this adventure would be your immediate domestic situation. What your re-actions would be to the rather senseless thoughts and talk being directed at your baby-body by your relatives and visiting admirers would be highly in-teresting but probably unsayable among thor-oughly nice people. Getting out of that situation and gaining your original poise would be an ad-venture all by itself. But, having accomplished this, it is fairly safe to assume that your next effort would be to try and discover more about the world you were in; what you were supposed to be doing in it; how you were related to the various objects about you; and, I suspect, why your relatives thought, talked, and behaved as they did in their watched and unwatched moments.

Taking all the borders from around our imagi-nations, let's pretend that you have decided to be-gin your research with the nearest thing at hand that looks interesting—your baby-body. Further-ing this supposition—and be sure to hold on to something for this one—let's say that the mental part of you has picked up the physical part of you, that is, your baby-body, and is about to examine it the way a jeweler examines a watch he has never looked into before. The surface inspection would be a brief one, for there wouldn't be much to look at. Inside the body, however, the examination would be more involved and more difficult, because of the multiplicity of mysterious-looking, delicately adjusted effects busily at work without union hours supposedly to keep that body alive and ticking according to regulation standards.

One of the important things you would have discovered if you had looked long and searchingly enough was that your little body, even while lying perfectly still, was filled to overflowing with harmony and rhythm. For you would have seen that every gadget and gear within that small skin-casing, down to the smallest whatsit, was not only functioning as a complete and distinct entity, but was blending and co-operating in the friendliest way with every other gadget, gear, and whatsit in the most perfect of orchestrations. Each specific item in that body, you would have learned, was in a state of spontaneous givingness, motivated by a power greater than its own. As you watched, you would have seen that each item was giving fully and freely of itself to all the other items in its vicinity, that the other items, in turn, were giving fully and freely of themselves to still more items, and so on and on, until these items formed the group of co-ordinating items called your human body.

With that illuminating illustration of individuality, altogetherness, and givingness to aid you,

you could then have set aside that small body, and have enlarged the focus of your interest until it took in the full sweep of your thinking areas. As you took a searching look around, you would have seen, first with curiosity, then with wonder, then with awe, and then with humble reverence, that back of your human, mistaken, misty sense of things everywhere was also making common cause with everything else, according to a perfect blueprint wherein there was but one cause, one plan, one purpose, many variations, but perfect unity.

From that point of vantage, high above the fogs of illusion and delusion common to the human species, you would have found yourself in direct contact with that for which men and women have been striving ever since time was invented—deathless, eternal REALITY. You would have been looking out upon, and at the same time have found yourself an integral part of, a universe of pure spirit. A universe in which everything was individualized and self-contained to the highest degree, but at the same time interrelated with everything else in perfect mutuality. A universe in which everything was drawing its life and intelligence from the same inexhaustible Source. A universe like a lovely, animated poem, in which the all-pervading Poet was continuously glorifying each individual, living expression, and each individual, living expression continuously glorifying the Poet, in endless combinations of form . . . color . . . melody . . . harmony . . . and rhythm.

*Chapter Eight*

## VERITIES

In the hectic struggle to maintain the *status quo* of three meals a day and one sleep—duo or solo— and to know just what to do with one's private assortment of ambitions, longings, vanity urges, and passions, there are four ancient verities that most human beings have a way of overlooking with almost flawless consistency. Verities so important to our well-being, happiness, and success that the failure to heed them, according to the world's greatest authorities, has been responsible for virtually all of our individual and collective woes. Permit me to set them down, as they are such splendid taking-off points for thumbing-out, rocking-chair adventures.

*The First:*    LIFE IS FOR LIVING.
*The Second:*  YOU CAN THINK.
*The Third:*   YOU HAVE BEEN PLACED IN CHARGE OF AN INDIVIDUAL LIFE, FOR WHICH YOU AND YOU ALONE ARE RESPONSIBLE.

*The Fourth:* YOU ARE EQUIPPED AND DESTINED
FOR UNLIMITED ACHIEVEMENT AND
BLESSEDNESS, YOUR ONLY BOUND-
ARIES BEING THOSE YOU SET FOR
YOURSELF OR PERMIT OTHERS TO SET
FOR YOU.

Looking at them casually on paper gives them
somewhat of a triteness, like those "wise sayings"
that many of us had to copy again and again after
school for some infraction of rules. But these
particular ones are well worth exploring for the
individual good tucked deep inside them. To
give you a somewhat different start into them, and
at the same time keep your fun faculties flexible, I
shall do what I did some chapters back: wave the
magic wand of make-believe in a certain secret
manner known only to relatively few grownups, reduce myself to the size of a Brownie, and straddle
the top of the page you are reading. And there
we are, let's say, you—the Big Shot of all you survey—and me—the little squirt who wrote the
book, looking across at you. A silly situation, of
course, but look about you! Then, before you
can decide what it's all about, I cup my hands and
shout across at you: "Hi there, my Hearty! Don't
forget that life is for living!"

It would be such a presumptuous greeting from

[55]

such an insignificant-looking little snip of an author that it is quite possible that you would be, shall we say, a trifle irked! And that, being irked, you would fling back at me something like this: "Thanks for the advice, which I did not ask for. Of course life is for living, everyone knows that. Why don't you say something original, if you're smart enough to squeeze yourself down to that ridiculous size and straddle book pages!"

To which I would reply in my best social manner, but with a well-concealed trap in every word: "Well, if life is for living and everyone knows it, how do you account for the fact that, either directly or indirectly, so many millions of people all over the earth are trying so hard to exterminate one another, not only physically, but socially, politically, economically, and what looks like every other kind of way?"

I wouldn't even try to guess what your answer might be to that one. But I certainly would like to be hidden back of one of your book ends, and listen to you explain this paradox in human behavior, or rather misbehavior, to a visitor from another planet who knew something about the perfection, harmony, and rhythm of real universal relations, and who had come over here by methods known only to himself to learn the reason for all the bad noise of strife and anguish coming from the planet Earth.

[56]

The probabilities are that trying to justify our individual and collective misconduct to such a universally minded guest would have left you limp and lateral even before you could get your vocal cords warmed up. For no matter how cleverly you maneuvered your theories and opinions, you would always be bumping into that unavoidable number one verity—that LIFE IS FOR LIVING.

The second and third verities: YOU CAN THINK, and YOU HAVE BEEN PLACED IN CHARGE OF AN INDIVIDUAL LIFE, FOR WHICH YOU AND YOU ALONE ARE RESPONSIBLE, are so closely related, we would agree, as almost to be one. They are rather obvious, but well worth exploring. Each of us, say the experts in these matters, is the captain and engineer of his own individual life, and so is strictly accountable for what he does with it. We can, if we choose, they point out, lay a wise and good course for ourselves, keep in the full stream of life and be a blessing to others all the way. Or we can shut off our engines—that is, our thinking—and float about with wind and current—a menace to navigation. Or we can anchor in some backwater to avoid effort and experience, and idly rot away. They are our lives and we are the ones who are thinking them around.

And speaking of thinking our individual lives around and being responsible for them, have you by chance noticed how far down in the scale of rational existence these same experts have been pegging the human species of late? Now, there's a prime scandal for you, considering the fact that we are supposed to be so incomparably superior in every point of living to all other organic forms of life on earth! What they are saying about an embarrassingly large percentage of us, what gives their rating that flavor of scandal, is that we have, they insist, become so flabby-minded from mental indolence that we have become easy push-overs for anyone who cares to come along, push us over, and count us.

Their main indictment against us is that, instead of fulfilling man's basic obligation to do his own thinking, we prefer turning this important function over to the control and management of others. All of which, they accusingly point out, is directly responsible for the shocking regimentation going on throughout the world in virtually every phase of human living. For the incredible number of slave mentalities. And particularly for the appalling number of amateur and professional dictators, racketeers, tyrants, demagogues, pretenders, rogues, and other slick defectives infesting almost every group activity from the smallest family to the largest nation.

It's a dark accusation against us, my Hearty! But then, let this be said too: you and I may sud-

denly discover ourselves in an enslavement of this
sort without having been aware that we were in
it, for these traps being mental, and so physically
unseen, are very subtle. Remembering those
second and third verities, however, all we have to
do is to start our mental engines, slip the anchor,
toot the whistle, and head outward with the best
compass directions we have on hand. It is as
simple as that, but it takes what seems like tremendous effort at first, much discipline, much courage,
and much daring. But it's well worth it!

The world's great thinkers, as you probably
know, have been thundering this and other truths
at us for centuries, trying in particular to make us
understand that nothing whatsoever can get into
one's individual living unless it first gets into his
individual thinking; and, getting into his individual thinking, is permitted to remain there.
Well do those clear-visioned ones know, and well
have they proved it too, that as individual thinking
moves, so, in turn, and with exact precision, move
the individual body, the individual experience,
and the individual environment. Like shadows
following the human body. "Therefore watch
your thinking!" they warn with every means at
their command. "Watch your thinking! Expand it Godward! Cherish it! Protect it! For
your thinking will head you toward all the heaven

you will ever know, but it will also head you into all the hell you experience! So watch your thinking!"

You would never have to call the attention of any of those great thinkers to that fourth verity, for most of them know that man, that is, the real man, is an illimitable spiritually mental being, an individualized idea, an immortal, and a celestial, here and now. That is why, you will note, they are always more interested in thoughts and thinking than in personalities, material things, and human events. Life, they would tell us, if we were ready for that knowledge—and Life to them is but another name for God—not only moves with us, but through us and as us. We are in It, they would point out, in It, and with It, and express It. As a drop of salt water containing all the ingredients of the ocean is in It, and with It, and expresses It. For a drop of salt water to say all by itself, "Here I am and here I come!" is one thing. But for that same drop to say, conscious of its oneness with the ocean, "Here WE come!" is something quite different.

So, regardless of what we may be doing, or seemingly be unable to do in everyday experience, there is always an out for us if we are looking for one, permit me to add before I flip off the top of this page and get out of my Brownie role. And it

[60]

doesn't in the least matter what others may be thinking or saying about us, or what we may be thinking and saying about ourselves; or about the degree of the darkness, discouragement, and futility that may have seeped into our outlook; for the perfect way of escape is ever at hand. And if you don't mind doing your own exploring, as I am having to do mine, you will find it perfectly set out, but embedded deep, in those four ancient verities: LIFE IS FOR LIVING . . . YOU CAN THINK . . . YOU HAVE BEEN PLACED IN CHARGE OF AN IN-DIVIDUAL LIFE, FOR WHICH YOU AND YOU ALONE ARE RESPONSIBLE . . . and YOU ARE EQUIPPED AND DESTINED FOR UNLIMITED ACHIEVEMENT AND BLES-SEDNESS, YOUR ONLY BOUNDARIES BEING THOSE YOU SET FOR YOURSELF OR PERMIT OTHERS TO SET FOR YOU.

[61]

*Chapter Nine*

## REFORMERS

Taking into consideration all the benefits be-
stowed upon every one of us by such a free-giving,
bountiful Creator, it seems almost incredible that
anyone should ever find existence either uninter-
esting or unprofitable.  If you have been finding
it so, the fault, according to both ancient and modern sages, does not lie in the circumstances that may
seem to be imprisoning you and cramping your
style; or with the personalities who may be both
in your hair and in your way; or with the bogies of
evil that throng your mental gloamings, and hiss,
threaten, and spit in your direction; but entirely
in your individual attitude toward these things.

Life, you couldn't very well help being aware,
if you read the newspapers, listen to the radio, or
observe what is going on about the earth, and in
your particular vicinity, hasn't been going any too
well for us human beings for a very considerable
time.  And speaking on the surface, at least, it
would seem to be getting steadily worse in spite
of all the efforts being made by well-intentioned

people to stop its deterioration. Other species riding the earth with us seem to be doing ever so much better, especially when it comes to such elemental things as getting satisfaction and happiness out of just being alive. Dogs for instance.

Of all the embarrassments common to the human species, none is more chronic than that of trying to explain why it is that, in a universe so overflowing with loveliness, goodness, abundance, and opportunity, so many countless millions upon millions of men, women, and children should be finding life so horribly and unnecessarily afflictive. Here we are, setting ourselves up as the top-ranking beings among the organic species, crediting ourselves with knowledge and understanding immeasurably beyond anything else with breath in it, supposed to be mental and moral pacesetters for the rest of creation; and yet if you and I were to search the earth at the present time, it is doubtful if we could find any other form of life behaving quite so stupidly, or so badly, or so selfishly, or so ruthlessly as our own. We'd have to come home and pin the blue ribbon for these qualities on ourselves.

Just why we human beings should display such relatively little talent for getting along with one another understandingly and helpfully, but so much for keeping the human family in continuous

[63]

disunity, enmity, and warfare, is something that students of the human scene have been trying to make sense of for a long time. Thinking one's way out into and then exploring this razzle-dazzle state of affairs in an effort to find the right answers is always a major rocking-chair adventure. Because of the rough and uncertain going, however, it is not adventuring for softies, or the timid, or the easily discouraged. In a geographical sense it would be the equivalent of setting out alone without map or compass to explore dense and undiscovered jungle country.

Reformers, both professional and amateur, militant and meek, ground and lofty, wise and otherwise, have been making this glaring flaw in our habits of behavior a point of attack for years. In fact, ever since that long-ago day when the first prehistoric man stopped long enough in the midst of what he should have been busy with, to fix an appraising and critical eye on his neighbor and decide he needed changing and regulating. Since then, as you must have noticed, this ambition to change and regulate the other fellow, and the other group, has developed into not only our most popular social pastime, but our Number One Industry.

Year after year, without even the grace of an occasional closed season, man has gone forth in ever-increasing numbers, usually filled with self-

[64]

righteous zeal, to change the thinking and actions of his fellow beings and make them conform more to his own.  Sometimes he has done this as a lone crusader, filled with stern fanaticism.  His more favored method, however, has been to gang up with as large a number of his own kind as possible, organize along political and military lines, and then with this display of size and power, bag as many converts as possible, not so much for the sake of the convert as for the prestige of the organization.

The panaceas offered by this array of reformers have been almost as numerous as the sands of the sea, and just about as varied too.  But while most of them differ in their public and private techniques for getting the results they are after, they are alike as peas in a pod in one thing, and that is in always aiming their reforming efforts at the other fellow, or the other group, and never at themselves.  Rarely do any of them attempt to influence others by trying to set them a good example.

And history records with shocking variations that the more man goes forth in his militantly minded, self-promoting way, to try and make over his fellow beings into the image and likeness of himself and then boss them around, the more obsessed he becomes with the notion that everyone

[65]

who doesn't think, speak, and act as he does is in the wrong and so an actual or potential enemy who needs corrective attention. Something, of course, has to happen with attitudes like that. And something did! There was an explosion! A spontaneous explosion of bad thinking! And the world found itself transformed into an arena for the greatest and most brutally savage free-for-all in human history. An arena in which neither rules nor regulations are recognized, and no slaughter methods barred.

That any light at all has penetrated into the din and blackness of this vast human befuddlement is due in large measure to our top-flight spiritual adventurers and explorers in different centuries who, usually alone, usually misunderstood, and usually unappreciated, have kept the Torch of Truth lighted, and moving from clean hand to clean hand, so to speak, in a glorious, unbroken chain. These illustrious men and women, ever moving against heavy odds, but never discouraged and never quitting, not only brought light into humanity's darkness, but were that light themselves, like undimable rays from an eternal, undimable Sun, giving luminosity and meaning to all things.

As one understandingly studies the lives of any of these luminous men and women, who put so much into human experience and ask for so little in return, he will make this interesting, and, I am sure, most helpful discovery: that every one of them places the emphasis of his living not on saying, or on doing, or on getting, or even on having, but almost entirely on BEING. That is the pivot for all their radiations, for all their great accomplishments. Their method is very simple. They live the best they know utterly, without reservations, and without compromise. And living thus in the full spread of their ever-expanding BEINGS, they not only enrich their own lives, but provide light, cheer, inspiration, courage, and good compass directions for all who ever came or who ever will come within the radius of their influence.

They are reformers too, but not in that manner wherein men, women, and children are maneuvered by one means or another into herds, branded, standardized, and then led about by their noses, or perhaps prodded from the rear. Their aim, one can easily learn from the things they say, write, and do, is to encourage the other fellow to want to get out of all entangling, limiting, individuality-crushing affiliations, and to show him how to get out of them in the most effective way. For with their knowledge, their far-reaching vision, and their richness of experience, they know that the

[67]

vital factor in all functioning throughout the universe is the individual unit; the individual unit complete within itself, true to its highest selfhood, and flowing along harmoniously, rhythmically, and contributively with all the others.

Reduced to its essence, what these clear-visioned men and women have been saying to the rest of us is this: "If you want the world to be a better place, stop trying to chip and carve others into what you think they should be like. Let them alone. Permit them to unfold in their own way and at their own rate of speed. And instead, go to work on yourself; you've got just about all the job you can attend to there. Reform yourself. Discipline yourself. Consecrate yourself to whatever you have before you to do, no matter how seemingly lowly and unimportant. When each of us succeeds in this, no other reformation will be necessary; for then the world will have been restored to its original purity, simplicity, and goodness, or Godlikeness; and each of us will find himself in Heaven—that is, a state of heavenly existence—without having to die to get there."

*Chapter Ten*

## ROCKING CHAIRS

There was a time, and not so very long ago, when philosophizing, which is but a high-hat and cutaway-coat term for mental adventuring and exploring, was a rather restricted activity and more or less limited to serious-faced, stiffish men who enthroned themselves on high but squeaking elevations, and then looked down at the passing throng with cold, analytical, calculating eyes, and that smugness that usually comes only from undue snootiness. Specialists they were, specialists who delved into the nature of and reason for things in a formalized way; used a ponderous jargon of their own; whacked one another with controversial phrases stiff enough to be used on the ends of polo mallets; and to pay for their rent, clothing, and groceries pronounced judgments on men and events for so much per lecture, per book, and per consultation.

The amateur at this sort of thing was not greatly encouraged, being needed for audience purposes. If he was brash enough to break loose from the particular herd with which he milled around, and say, write, invent, compose, or otherwise do something really original, he was apt to be set upon, at least mentally, vocally, and socially, by hordes of what the kindlier expositors call latent and slow developers. By that description they mean those who contribute very little toward keeping life humming and happy, and are always opposed to change and expansion for themselves or anyone else. Organized ignorance in particular would have clipped at him, organized ignorance with its dictatorial power and its ever-continuous effort to strip man of his birthright of individuality and initiative, and keep him buried and submissive in the regimented mass mind and the regimented mass action.

The operation of this sort of thing may be amusingly illustrated by using as an analogy one of those old-fashioned, New England, public-school dancing classes that many of us had to attend when we were young and unable to avoid such things. Reproduced today they would appear as comedy bordering on burlesque; as a matter of fact, they were just about that then. Here is the picture: a large, cheerless room that the school board didn't consider worth decorating; a venerable, upright piano that probably came over on the *Mayflower,* with an oldish sourpuss sitting

[70]

in front of it; and filling the rest of the scene a martinet in the form of a spinster-teacher, armed with a rattan stick that she used as a sort of combination baton and bayonet.

In that forbidding atmosphere, we kids would be lined up like convicts, given strict orders, and then, led by one of her pets, set to snaking around the room in a dreary one-two-three-and-dip! one-two-three-and-dip! Every step and dip of the way that sharp voice barked at us, trying to make all of us do the same thing at the same time. Now and then we would be commanded to stop, turn in her direction, curtsey and bow, as a forced tribute to her, I suppose, and then back again we'd go into that monotonous one-two-three-and-dip! one-two-three-and-dip! What it was all about was a secret none of us discovered. But one thing we did know, that swift punishment ranging all the way from a prod with that rattan stick to banishment in disgrace from the class awaited any one of us who deliberately or unintentionally dipped a beat ahead of the others, a beat behind them, or, most reprehensible of all, didn't dip at all.

From one point of view it is an amusing experience to look back upon, but from another it is tragic. For, mark you this, out of millions upon millions of seemingly minor episodes like that dancing class, episodes in which some minor tyrant

[71]

has sought to mass, mold, and dominate others, instead of trying to set their individualities free so that they could be themselves and express themselves for the good of all, have blossomed most of our present-day evils.    And particularly such evils as our sinister herd standards . . . our mental and physical goose-stepping . . . our class conflict . . . our cramped, dreary lives . . . our narrowness of outlook . . . our exclusiveness . . . our intolerance . . . our ill will . . . our selfishness . . . our greed . . . our violent epidemic of disunity . . . and our disappointing, decadent, tottering human civilization.

As mentioned before, but worth repeating again because of its far-reaching implications, when this amateurishly managed human world of ours blew out more than its customary number of moral fuses some time back and we found ourselves involved in the inferno of another world war, each of us was forced to become a mental explorer whether he wanted to do so or not; owing principally to the fact that the cataclysm was so terrifying, so baffling, so intimately personal.

Those wise ones who really understood the reason for it all had no illusions as to who or what was to blame for the bad world conditions.  They threw the responsibility right into the lap of the individual human being, pointing out as they did so that the world couldn't possibly improve until the individual himself improved; and that the individual himself couldn't improve until he first improved the quality of his thinking; until he gave himself a thorough overhauling inwardly, and then mentally headed out in the direction of his highest levels.

Now when it comes to moving out toward one's higher levels—which of course is mental adventure and exploration—there are two different schools of thought as to just what one should do with his physical body upon such expeditions. One of them favors keeping the body as inactive as possible. The other advocates keeping the body active. The adherents of the inactive school believe that the more they think about their human bodies and indulge them, the more they are handicapped in getting about mentally and spiritually. So they place their bodies in whatever position they most favor, make them as motionless as possible, forget them, and then move out mentally into their larger body or area of consciousness.

The advocates of the other school, equally interested in exploring the invisible and unknown, regard motion as synonymous with Life. Consequently, they believe that new ideas come more spontaneously when one's whole being, physical as well as mental, is in movement. So, instead of making their bodies inert when they go mental-adventuring, they keep them in a state of constant activity. Some, for instance, achieve their aims by walking their bodies through lovely scenery. Others prefer moving their physicality through space on the back of a horse, the deck of a boat, in a train, a plane, an automobile, or working at some agreeable occupation, like gardening.

If you are in any doubt as to which of these methods would suit you best for private mental exploring, let me suggest that you try the rocking-chair method. There are a number of advantages in this method, not the least of them being that with the rocking chair you can straddle both schools of thought and at the same time get the most excellent results. But if you decide to do this, let me warn you of the importance of coming seat-to-seat with a rocking chair that not only counterbalances your particular style of chassis, but your particular style of mind, feelings, emotions, yearnings, and sentiments as well.

Rocking chairs, you will come to discover, have just as definite individualities, characters, and temperaments as human beings. And they can be just as moody and ornery too. For instance, some of these chairs fiddle-faddle back and forth, stiff with pride, petulance, and pretense, like certain people each of us knows and wishes he didn't. Beware of them!   Then there is that voguish type, the last word in commercial modernism, with plenty of flash and sparkle but little character and less rhythm, having been made without inspiration, enthusiasm, or affection.   And then there are those hastily slapped-together, antisocial specimens—chairs that hold human bodies grudgingly, as though they'd like nothing better than dumping their occupants over backward as a mark of their thorough disapproval of the human species both collectively and individually.   By all means keep away from them!

The best kind of a rocking chair for mental exploring is one that was made by an understanding mind and friendly, sensitive hands.   Every chair of this kind that I have rocked in had been thought and wrought into human visibility by poets who used wood as their medium of expression instead of words.   They were poets who, through consecration to their particular talent, first turned themselves into an animated poem, and then flowed full and free into what eventually became a lovely rocking chair.   They did this as the earth's great thinkers and sharers flowed into literature, or art, or music, or, most difficult of all, Life itself.   Their rocking chairs had in them everything a good rocking chair should have:

[75]

character . . . simplicity . . . proportion . . . balance . . . cadence . . . the gentleness of a cradle . . . the promise of friendliness, tranquillity, and repose . . . and in their movement something of the stately, reassuring, deep ticktocking swing of a well-balanced pendulum, in a time-giving but time-defying old grandfather's clock.

*Chapter Eleven*

## BEING

Fantasy is so interwoven into the very warp and woof of everyday experience that even those professionals who devote their time to delving into the conscious and so-called subconscious sectors of the human mind, and out of them try to classify and explain for the general public mental functions and human behavior, are forced time and time again to try and puzzle out for their own private information just where what they term actuality really leaves off and fantasy really begins. And not only that, but where to place the correct dividing line between wisdom and folly, sanity and insanity, genius and eccentricity, good and evil, right and wrong, life and death, and all those other contradictions so disturbing to the human species. In their efforts to achieve this clarity, they are often like small boys playing mumble-the-peg, as they fling an open jackknife backward over their heads, hoping that where it sticks in is where it ought to be.

With this comparison in mind, it is interesting

to ponder what might happen to this overregimented, unhappy world of ours if every citizen in every country were to devote a couple of early morning or late evening hours to independent mental exploration. To placing his body in a rocking chair, let's say, and then with his thumbprint to remind him of his real individuality and universal importance, moving out into the greatest of all adventures: that of searching within himself to find himself, so that he can know himself, and in that knowing of himself, be himself, and in that being of himself, share himself with whoever or whatever needs what he has to offer.

In these days of stark, materialistic realism, when ruthless, competitive existence is at an unusually high peak, such a suggestion may sound rather frivolous, like a waste of both time and effort. But if you will look back through the pages of history, you will discover that this particular type of individual mental exploring, even though carried on without the aid of a rocking chair, was responsible for bringing into human experience virtually all the good things we are enjoying today. Someone was always thinking out, finding, coming back, and sharing. You could, if you preferred, call such exploring prayer, as so many do. Or meditation. Or speculation. Or realization. Or introspection. Or cogitation.

Or affirmation and denial. Or contemplation. Or just plain, ordinary thinking things through.

I like the term mental adventuring and exploring, because it is so vital, so expressive, so unlimiting, so individual, and so shot full of meaning. Thinking of it in these terms helps me to keep the entire activity free, spontaneous, and fluid. To keep it away from that orthodox insincerity and pretense. To keep it away, too, from those humanly designed, antiquated thought-forms that weren't provable even when first advanced; and especially from all those organized and controlled influences that would stifle individual thinking and expression.

To all men and women with aliveness, who are ever eager to know more, see more, experience more, and thus live more abundantly, as all the ancient Bible writers assured us each of us was entitled to do throughout time and eternity, there is an exhilarating tang and challenge in that term mental adventuring and exploring. They may not at first be able to grasp the tremendous personal significance of it, but they can feel its attraction; and in that feeling become responsive to the tug and pull of an unseen Something ever taking them into larger areas of themselves.

To be successful at this kind of adventuring and exploring one has to make the strictest demands upon himself. His code, of necessity, is a strict one. It demands of him, first of all, that, come what may, he will be true to his highest selfhood. He has to quit drifting with popular emotional crowd-currents. He has to stop depending upon others to tell him what he should think and when, and what he should do and how. He conditions himself to do his own thinking at all times, and extends the same privilege to all others, ever knowing that right thinking and impersonal thinking always blend and harmonize. He is eager to share and co-operate, but he refuses to be controlled, dominated, or intimidated by anyone or anything.

Being an adventurer and interested in discovering as many new facets of Truth as possible, he is willing to take chances in experimenting with Life, provided those experiments lead in the direction of some promised good for all. And he is willing to attempt the difficult task of blazing new trails through the dense jungles of human ignorance and stupidity, even though he knows them to be filled with hostile Indians. He learns in this trial-and-error experience, which all of us seem to have to go through, that mistakes are more or less unavoidable until one achieves the ultimate perfection. So he makes his mistakes, but stays in them only long enough to extract the needed lesson and blessing; and then proceeds on his way again with new spirit and determination, undiscouraged by the failures, and undisturbed by either misjudgment or criticism.

Real mental adventuring and exploring is not easy, my Hearty, as many superlative men and women have discovered in every age. As a matter of fact, this poking around all alone in the unfamiliar regions of one's own mind, or world of consciousness, is so filled with sudden and most unexpected adventure, and the back country of one's mind, or world of consciousness, is so trackless, so uncharted, and so mysterious that even having the courage to attempt it is enough to entitle one to a special medal for distinguished endeavor.

Ventures of this kind demand individual thinking at its individual best, which probably explains why there are not more great mental adventurers and explorers around. As has been observed before, Mr. Average Citizen, wherever he walks the earth, does not take to original thinking any too easily or too willingly. When he can be lured or prodded into it, he invariably finds the experience highly satisfying and beneficial. But thinking—that is, real, individual thinking—requires exertion. And on top of exertion, discipline. And on top of discipline, perseverance. And for the average person predigested, canned thoughts seem to be much easier to swallow. At least they used to be when the world was in a happier and more orderly mood. Today, however, these canned thoughts have a decided tendency to give people acute mental indigestion, usually followed by great confusion, discouragement, and distress.

The mental adventurer and explorer is always equipped with certain fundamental facts about Life—not just life—that are of the greatest help to him as he starts out on his ventures. One of them is this: that Life is immeasurably greater than all its definitions and descriptions. Another: that Life, really being mental and spiritual, cannot possibly be limited to a brief stretch of time between a humanly established point called birth and another humanly established point called death. And because he is aware of these great Truths, he knows that Life, in spite of every appearance to the contrary, is unending . . . ever-unfolding . . . lovely . . . friendly . . . co-operative . . . beneficial . . . delightful . . . and altogether good. But he also knows that Life doesn't hang around and wait for anyone; that Life demands action, demands living, demands the fullest co-operation. So he flings all of himself into It, and moves along with It.

His main object is integration. To find his individual spiritual identity and be it to the utmost

[82]

and in this effort to interblend his all with that of all other individual spiritual identities in the eternal and forever Oneness and Allness of Creation. He must, he knows, constantly be his part in the life that is Life. And so, realizing that the Cause of all must of necessity be wise and good, he looks for wisdom and goodness in every person, thing, situation, and condition he encounters. In this way, with here a little gained and there a little gained, and experiencing both defeats and triumphs, he comes at last into demonstrable relations with that for which mankind has ever sought: reality—the reality behind all the signs, symbols, and names.

Through this individual mental exploring, he learns one of Life's most precious lessons: namely, how to BE what he divinely is, always has been, and always will be. And in that BEing, he finds that his DOing becomes natural, spontaneous, productive, contributive, and satisfying. It has to be like that, he learns, for it is divine law. And as he keeps mentally alert, progressive, and receptive, he begins to see more and more clearly that the creative, governing Mind and Energy that keeps the stars in their courses is moving full time with him, and giving him in unlimited abundance all the life, wisdom, guidance, co-operation, good, happiness, and success he can possibly use.

[83]

*Chapter Twelve*

## BUGGING AROUND

We had just finished dinner on the terrace of a quaint, old, story-bookish inn, in a quaint, old, story-bookish village in the South of France, a bit of the world that human beings can never damage to any great extent, however violent their emotions, because of the enduring loveliness of earth and sea and sky. My companion was an old and much-admired friend who had been almost everywhere that men like to go and was just as accomplished a mental explorer as he was a geographer. The night was soft and fragrant with salt air and the pungent smell of growing things. Between us was a dinner table covered with a still spotless white cloth from which a quaint, old, story-bookish waiter had just removed the dishes. Below us, shimmering under a yellow moon, was the Mediterranean Sea in one of its most seductive moods.

For some time we had been talking about life as each of us had been experiencing it in various parts of the world since we had last met. It was good talk, especially from his side, as he had a rare blending of intelligence, humor, and discriminating appreciation, and was a splendid conversationalist in any kind of company. Knowing his capacity for saying the unexpected, I asked him what he thought it was, basically, that made us humans, with all our advantages and the things we are supposed to know, mess up life so consistently and thoroughly, especially our relations with one another. With his background it was a perfect target for him to shoot at.

He half closed his eyes into a characteristic squint, as though getting a range on the target, and began tapping his nose slowly with one of his fingers, which was always a sign that mental ammunition of heavy caliber was coming up his hoist. But before he could fire there was an interruption. A little bug, looking as though he had just come out of a bottle of ink, crawled over the rim of the table between us, paused to survey the terrain, and then, in a most stately manner for a little bug, started for the other side. He was so black and the tablecloth so white that he looked almost twice his size, which no doubt was the impression he wished to create. My friend, with his customary swift co-ordination of thought and action, pulled a thick-leaded pencil from his pocket and made a circle on the cloth around the little fellow.

[85]

The bug went marching along until he came to the pencil mark. Then he stopped abruptly. For some time he stood there perfectly still, evidently trying to figure out what he had suddenly come up against. It finally seemed to occur to him that the black thing looming up ahead was a high and impassable barrier, for he turned and hurried obliquely to the left. Again the barrier! He tried in another direction, then another, and and another, but always that thing was in his way. Eventually he apparently got the notion that he was trapped, for he started racing around in a meaningless way, in a frenzy of fear. Finally, either because he was dizzy, worn out, or utterly discouraged, he stopped in the center of the circle and became as motionless as the table.

My friend and I watched the performance with amusement, wondering what, if anything, he would do next. There was no next, he was through, he had quit cold. My friend laid the end of his pencil against the little fellow's rear end and gently pushed him outside the circle. He lay there without any trace of life for some seconds. Then he sensed a change in the situation, for he pushed his chassis up as high as it would go, turned around a few times to convince himself that he was still intact, and then raced across the table and disappeared. My guess was that he was hurrying home to warn his relatives and friends to keep away from white-topped tables where human giants face one another, and, while making horrible noises through holes in their heads, spring enormous black traps around respectable bugs going about their own business.

I didn't get my friend's reactions to the performance, because he was suddenly called away; but to me it was as funny an episode as I had come upon in a long time. But as I chuckled about it I wondered seriously how anything capable of expressing life and of moving its body around with the facility of that bug could possibly be so stupid as to believe that anything so obviously flat as a circle made with a lead pencil could stop anything. It was not only stupid, I decided, but an all-time low in stupidity. But as I came to this conclusion I began sensing in a vague sort of way that something in connection with that bug and the circle had a direct bearing on the question I had asked my friend.

Sitting there alone, looking out into all that loveliness, and letting my thoughts flit, flutter, and float where they pleased, it occurred to me with somewhat of a shock that I had no right to assume a smug, overweening attitude toward that little bug and his frightened efforts to get out of that circle; nor to look so arrogantly down my nose and

[87]

laugh at him as a deficient expression of life. For I myself, I suddenly became aware, had done virtually the same thing times without number; had run around senselessly and even stupidly, too, in what in my world was the equivalent of pencil-mark circles.

Most of mine had been invisible circles, to be sure, but they had imprisoned me as successfully for the time being as that pencil-circle had stopped the little bug. They were circles I had drawn around myself and my activities, or circles I had permitted others and circumstances to make around me. Circles of limitation and frustration. Circles in which, like the little bug, I too whirled and swirled, hot and bothered, confused and dizzy, baffled and discouraged, getting nowhere, and accomplishing less. But there seemed to be more excuse for the little bug, for I was supposed to be so much higher up in the scale of intelligence. And was my face red in that yellow moonlight!

But I did not allow my embarrassment to discourage me too much, either emotionally or philosophically, the night being far too enchanting for that. And besides, there was bubbling up within me a rather sardonic satisfaction in recalling that almost everyone I knew was bugging around in some kind of a circle too. Circles of temporarily arrested being, of arrested doing, of arrested ex-

[88]

perience, of arrested almost everything within the bounds of human experience. And the spinners-around in them as trapped, and as stopped in their hopes, plans, and purposes as that little bug within the pencil marks. And no more so.

I didn't quit the adventure there—it was far too interesting and revealing. And the more I explored into the thing, the more apparent it became where most of our human trials and troubles, headaches and heartaches, wants and woes, frustrations and failures, and disappointments and disillusionments were coming from. It was becoming clearer in every mental direction. They were coming from a major but common error with two prongs on it. One prong was individual failure to evaluate correctly the purpose of Life and one's place in it; and the other, the needless bugging around in purely imaginary circles that most of us accept as real.

Thanks to a lot of indirect help from that little bug, with his faulty observation and mistaken beliefs, what I was discovering inwardly while bathing outwardly in that gorgeous atmosphere was tremendously revealing, but by no means new. For the more I thought about it, the more I was able to recall that many of the world's greatest thinkers had sent out specific warnings against the use of tags of limitation, personally or otherwise.

[89]

Warnings against attempting to hinder in any way the motion or action of any expression of Life, especially one's own. Warnings against trying to deprive any living thing of its liberty and happiness, or of permitting one's self to be robbed of them. And then I blushed for all of us in that yellow moonlight.

*Chapter Thirteen*

## ENCIRCLEMENTS

As your eyes come onto this page with, I hope, your thinking still functioning in a fluid and adventurous way, may I suggest that you take off your shoes, if you have any on, wiggle your toes, and while this pleasant operation is going on give yourself an old-fashioned, seventh-inning stretching! You will find it agreeably relaxing, and in that untensing you should discover that your thinking has broken over its customary bounds and is spreading itself to most unusual proportions.   And not only that, but that all about you, or, more correctly, within you, new ideas are beginning to pop like good corn over a hot fire.

Then, when you feel at peace with your universe—that is, your mental awareness of it—try this by way of a personal adventure: Swing your mental antenna around and then in a searching but friendly way tap back through experience and note how much of your time and effort have been given either to spinning around submissively within limited encirclements or to trying to get yourself out of them. Encirclements around your thinking . . . your capacities . . . the fulfillment of your hopes, ambitions, and dreams . . . your relations with other people . . . your work . . . your opportunities . . . your happiness . . . your peace of mind . . . in fact, around almost every phase of your everyday existence. Encirclements imprisoning you like the little bug in the last chapter. Encirclements that, for at least a time, restricted you, embarrassed you, discouraged you, and bluffed you into believing that escape into larger areas of happiness, accomplishment, and usefulness was impossible.

You'll probably find lots of them, but don't let that discourage you in the least, for we all have been rimmed, and still are rimmed in varying degrees, with these arresting impositions. Which probably explains why we are still only human beings in the process of evolution, instead of celestials enjoying the freedom and ecstasy of all that really is. You will find some highly profitable adventure by exploring into the reasons for these encirclements, especially if you broaden the scope of it by reading or thinking back through history and observing with what enthusiasm we humans have gone in for making and maintaining encirclements around ourselves. Doing so, you will particularly note how we split ourselves into all kinds of antagonistic national, racial, social, religious, and political groupings; and then shut ourselves off from one another by narrow, heavily guarded drawbridges over otherwise uncrossable moats.

As you ponder this behavior, for whatever help it may be to you and those with whom you share yourself, you should make all sorts of new and interesting discoveries with that adventuring and expanding point of view of yours; and remember that adventuring and expanding point of view of yours is desperately needed by your world right now. One of the things you will come upon that should both interest and shock you is the thoughtless and damaging part you may have unintentionally been playing in the diabolical mass effort to make omnipresent and interrelated Life function on a framework of division, separation, difference, and exclusion.

Some of the most competent authorities in these matters point to these differences as our most ancient and vicious mass futility, adding in no uncertain terms that when it comes to understanding the plan and purpose of Life and fitting ourselves into its functions in an intelligent way, we humans, taking us as a whole, are so backward as to be only a few notches above zero in the universal scale of existence. Now, how do you like that, my Hearty?

[93]

If, through pride in your species, or perhaps your personal vanity, you should disagree with this sweeping indictment, or wish to argue the point with the authorities, they would, I feel sure, smile at you in a kindly but indulgent way, as though you were a small child, and gently suggest that you take a look at the current human scene, or do some reading of history.

One of the gravest faults in connection with this weakness, these experts say, is not so much the limiting encirclements we put around ourselves and others and allow others to put around us, but rather our disinclination to get out of them and into larger and more useful orbits of living. We like encirclements, they insist. Like to wall ourselves in behind traditions, prejudices, ignorance, customs, habits, and all sorts of other things. And having done this, to let the rest of the world shift for itself, without any interest, affection, or co-operation from us. We are afraid of change, they charge, afraid of expanding, afraid of the unfamiliar, scared stiff at new ideas; we prefer to stay in the ruts and routines of our particular family, group, gang, crowd, or mob, and let someone boss us around.

But they don't let the indictment rest, even there. They charge, with all the impact of a well-flung harpoon, that whenever the average human

[94]

being is biologically comfortable, feels reasonably secure, and is enjoying his quota of animal pleasures, he—figuratively at least—squats where he is, snaps a padlock on his mind, and starts to vegetate. If he moves about at all, they continue with sharpened irony, he usually does so in a popular encirclement bounded on the north by I, on the east by MY, on the south by ME, and on the west by MINE. An encirclement lined with mirrors and sound amplifiers wherein he can be the big frog in a little puddle, and watch himself perform and listen to himself croak at one and the same time. Well-frogs, they call us, well-frogs satisfied with our encircling walls and narrow boundaries, and not the least bit interested in great oceans or the rivers that flow into them.

Amazing phenomena these encirclements, from whatever angle you look! I don't know if you can recall your first encirclement, but I can recall mine. It happened in a kindergarten in the historical, old city of Newport, Rhode Island. Educationally speaking, it was an exceptionally fine kindergarten, but to me it was merely an enlargement of my own pleasant family, a place in which everyone and everything existed for only one purpose, as I believed, and that was to provide me with a good time and keep my masculine ego inflated. It was a delightful and irresponsible

[95]

stretch of existence, filled with fun, wonderment, and glad surprises.

Education there was as it should be: simple, easy to grasp, adaptable to what was at hand, and always with a kindly and festive touch to it. We were taught by teachers who not only loved us, but liked us, which made it easy for all of us. Within the first month I had become the undisputed champion at sewing pencil-outlined elephants on cardboard with bright-colored yarn. Not much to brag about now, but enough at the time to make me a big shot in the class. And so life flowed along like the proverbial song. At least it did until a certain fateful day when the arch enemy of all young life, the Board of Education, decided that the time had come for us kids to leave kindergarten and begin doing time at hard labor in the grade schools.

It was a tragic occasion. Without either consultation or warning, we were lined up, marched out, and herded together in the first of the grade schools. The others—all of them I suddenly discovered were sissies—capitulated. But not I. I rebelled. I didn't like the grade school, the teacher, or the things she proposed to teach me. Nor did I fall for the salestalk she gave me about being able to make me President of the United States, if I would behave like the others and do what she told me to do. I didn't want to become President of the United States, and I didn't want any more education. I had had enough. And besides, was I not the champion at sewing outlined elephants on cardboard with colored yarn, and one of the big shots in the kindergarten?

When no one was watching I sneaked back to the kindergarten. I didn't stay long; they strong-armed me back to the grade school. The next day I went back to the kindergarten again, and the next day, and the day after that, until I became a problem and a headache for quite an assortment of relatives and educators. In the end their side won, but only because they had the most numbers and the best strategy on their side. But it took their combined efforts, and if I had had a little more knowledge it would have taken the army and navy too to wean me away from that kindergarten.

Today I am most grateful to them all, for if I had been permitted to have my own way, I would in all probability still be in that kindergarten, sewing outlined elephants on cardboard with bright-colored yarn. It was, in a certain sense of things, an encirclement not greatly unlike the one in which the little bug found himself; but with this difference, the little bug wanted to get out of his, and I didn't. I would have been satisfied to have vegetated indefinitely in that kindergarten, and to have let Life move on without me. But Life, I subsequently had to learn, doesn't permit that. One either moves along with It, or is disciplined in some form or other until one does.

*Chapter Fourteen*

## MARGINS

If I didn't feel obligated to sit here in the patterned shade of this heavily fruited lemon tree in this old California garden, and angle for upstream swimming ideas with which to finish the rest of the book you are now trailing me through, do you know what I would like to do on this impeccable Spring morning?  Roll a piano out here into all this loveliness and spend the next few hours, or days, or even centuries if necessary—for what is time among Immortals?—with my fingers on the black keys, the ones with which I get the best results, composing a rocking-song for the human species.

There is an abundance of action-songs available today, but relatively few rocking-songs.  The only ones I can recall offhand are a number written long, long ago for babies; that old salty one that bass singers loved to bellow once upon a time, about "lying down" and being "rocked in the cradle of the deep"; and a brimstony one that a rootin-tootin, son-of-a-gun of a cowboy friend of mine likes to sing whenever he contemplates throwing a rock or two at people he regards as inferior. My ambition is to fashion a song that can either be sung vocally or thought without utterance as one's physical body rides in a rocking chair and his thinking gallops high, wide, and handsome all over his imagination, on the trail of more satisfying answers to the ever-challenging questions of WHY? and HOW? and WHEN?

The song I have in mind, if I can only get it out from where it seems to be to where I should like to see it be, is a new all-out design in harmonic rhythm, and will be arranged not only for the vocal cords but for one's entire being, the rocking chair, and even the Universe itself. It will be a rollicking sort of song, filled with exhilaration, inspiration, good sense, fun, bounce, and boom-ta-rah! And it will be saturated with a free and understanding camaraderie for everything everywhere. It has no title. I have in mind leaving that a blank so that each one can write his own, and thus be a kind of partner in the enterprise. But the refrain of it will swing along something like this: "Margins! Margins! Margins! Rocking out of Margins, Margins, Margins!"

If it doesn't go over very well with the public at large—and that is a definite possibility, unless I substitute for the rocking chair a swaying love seat and sugar the song up sentimentally for highly emotionalized couples—it might have a chance as a theme song for The Unorganized League of Rocking-chair Adventurers and Explorers. They've never had a theme song, not even a bad one. And they really need one, for the members are always trying to rock themselves out of margins of one kind or another—margins that the human mass mind with its limited and misty, low visibility has placed around almost everything it can identify in its vain effort to break up the Oneness and Infinitude of Creation into little, detached, isolated pieces, and make the pieces fit into private plans.

Now a margin, according to Mr. Webster and his associates, is "a condition approximately marking the limit at which something will remain or continue to be or act . . . a limit beyond which change cannot take place without a cessation of certain activities and phenomena." As something merely to read in these superexciting days, that definition may sound a bit dull. But if you will read it both thoughtfully and with your intake wide open, keeping in mind some of those visible and invisible barriers that may be shutting you off from the things you would like to experience, accomplish, and have, you will be surprised at how much of you is involved in it.

It may interest you to know that the expert observers and interpreters of the human scene are greatly alarmed over this question of margins. And they are alarmed because the more they study individual and collective human behavior, both in its inward and outward phases, the more intensely do they insist that the margins we humans as a whole have placed around our thinking and our doing are directly responsible for most of our militantly unsocial attitudes and emotions . . . our ruthless competition . . . our greed . . . our acquisitiveness . . . our strife . . . our wars . . . our want . . . our woe . . . and our bitter wretchedness.

The situation is critically serious, they all agree, but not irreparable. Like all men with vision and balance, they have a solution for the difficulty. And here it is, reduced to the proverbial nutshell: If the world is ever to be taken out of the deplorable state into which each of us, either directly or indirectly, has helped plunge it, and restored to its original perfection and blessedness, each of us must immediately break through his margins of ingrowing exclusiveness and selfishness, recognize his personal responsibility as a citizen of the universe, and do something about it . . . not only now, but in an ever-continuing series of nows.

Aristotle, who was one of the most famous of all the mental adventurers and explorers, once said:

"A thing is only at its best when it is becoming that of which it is capable." Instead of taking such an excellent observation to heart, however, and trying consistently to live up to the best one knows moment by moment, mankind seems generally to use its becomingness as a kind of mattress of hope on which to repose indolently, and, while wishing for the best, expect the worst. Well did Aristotle know that men and women can find true happiness and success only by ceaselessly improving themselves, by expanding themselves, and by sharing themselves. But he also knew, through that penetrating vision of his, how prone the average human being is to crowd himself into the confines of narrow, self-centered margins, and then stagnate mentally, spiritually, and finally, of course, physically.

Three friends of mine well illustrate the latter process, and I'd like to give you a peek at them. All three are from what the blue books would term good families, and all three have college degrees, which are supposed to mean that they were turned loose in the world equipped to be of superior service to their fellows. The first was a nationally known football star for three seasons. He now works at a job that a horse could do just about as well if it had hands and a union card. It is a job requiring little intelligence but much physical application; consequently he does little original thinking either at work or away from it. His mental, spiritual, and physical margins are unbelievably circumscribed; his interests rarely extend beyond his biological needs and urges. Others make up his mind for him and tell him what to do. He's hefty and healthy and he moves about, but a modern diagnostician would probably decide that he is just about as dead as he ever will be, and is merely waiting for something to resurrect him into a higher state of being.

My second friend is a minor official in a major corporation, an organization in which everyone thinks and acts so much alike that they all more or less look alike. He is fond of boasting that he is just like his father and his grandfather in almost everything from attitudes and mannerisms to religion and politics. His granite-like margins are bounded by his particular ancestors, his particular family, his particular job, his particular form of organized religion, his particular political party, his particular fraternal organization, and his particular two-weeks-vacation place, the same one he has been going to ever since he was a boy. Within these narrow margins he struts like a bantam rooster. If he looks beyond these bounds, he instantly becomes suspicious, unfriendly, prejudiced, hostile, and murderous and destructive, at least mentally. As far as any universal usefulness is concerned, he, too, would probably be listed with the walking-talking dead.

The third man is a great success, strictly materially speaking. He is a wizard in high finance and promotion or one of the slickest big-time criminals not yet behind prison bars, according to the way one looks at these things. He lives in a world of bluff, bluster, and insincerity. A world in which everyone gives as little as he has to, and grabs all he can, as in strip poker. It is a ruthless world in which humans prey on one another, not because of any real need, but solely to satisfy personal abnormalities in the form of vanity, greed, ambition, and lust for power. It is a world in which no one ever asks: "How did you win?" but only: "Did you win?" By outsmarting and outpreying others he has acquired an abundance of things. But he might just as well not have them, because he has no opportunities for really enjoying them. He has no friends, in the best meaning of that term, no peace of mind, no contentment, and no one, as far as I know, whom he dares trust. He has trapped himself in the ever-narrowing, crushing margins of his own selfish, acquisitive racket.

Three innately fine fellows with great latent capacities for helping to make the world better, happier, and more interesting for others. But

three innately fine fellows contributing generously
to the general delinquency of the human species
by refusing to come out of their selfish margins,
either understandingly, sympathetically, or co-op-
eratively.

Three innately fine fellows serving sentences at
hard labor in invisible prisons of their own making.   Three innately fine fellows living in a world
of limitless beauty, goodness, friendliness, and
never-ending delights, but almost totally unaware
of it!

Three innately fine fellows who, with all their
educational equipment and opportunities for observation, have never learned one of the most
basic and important facts about Life: namely, that
thought externalizes itself according to undeviating law, the undeviating law of like always producing like.   If they had been able to discover
that somewhere along the line, they would have
known that their physical bodies, their environment, their relationships, their experiences, in
fact, everything having to do with their world,
were simply the outward expression, or the pressing out of their thinking.   And knowing that,
each of them could have thought his world back
into its original state of perfection, and have been
able to keep it there.

But there is hope for my friends, for while they

are shut in by their margins, they are not locked in. And neither are you, my Hearty, no matter how high, narrow, or arresting your present margins may seem to be.

*Chapter Fifteen*

## SCAPEGOATS

Two obvious truisms begin this chapter. The first, that each of us has just about all he can attend to in trying to manage his own day-and-nightness in a decent and respectable way. And the second, that no one has the right to look uncharitably down his nose at his neighbor, especially in these grim times of social and economic levelings, or to make blueprints for his neighbor's life, or even, as a general rule, to tell him what to do. And while I try to subscribe to these precepts, with not too great success much of the time, I want to attempt a kind of sneak-through them, so that you can have another look at those three friends of mine mentioned in the last chapter; the object being, to see if we can find anything further in their patterns of living that will be useful warnings to us in these difficult, unpredictable days.

To do this effectively but differently, I shall waive conventional procedure and drag them into these pages as scapegoats, something after the method used by the ancients with the four-legged variety.   Now, those ancients, you will recall from your Bible history, became acutely aware at frequent intervals of their sins of omission and commission, even as you and I.   And this awareness, it would appear, came not so much from an individual and collective desire to be more ethical, and to express more good in their relations with one another as it did from the afflictive and distressing things their sins of omission and commission were doing to them.   Their remedy was original and unique, to say the least.   They would go into the wilderness, capture a goat, take it to the appointed place, ceremoniously dump all their sins upon its head, turn it loose again in the wilderness, and then go on from where they left off.

I am attempting a modernistic adaptation of this idea, using my three friends as the scapegoats and inviting you to join me in hypothetically dumping all our personal sins of omission and commission upon their heads.   Then we can hypothetically turn them loose again into whatever wilderness is handy with a formal nod of appreciation and a squirt or two of perfume, to show them no malice was intended.   So, for the fun of the experiment, and, of course, for whatever good we may get out of it, let's pretend that my three friends are on individual exhibition platforms like those used in circus sideshows, where we can stare at them, poke them, talk about them, and say things at them without their having an opportunity to come back at us.

Having known them for some time, I feel sure I am safe in saying that, after you had observed them at close range for a while, you wouldn't— from personal desire—choose any one of them as a dinner companion, unless you were starving or needed a very special favor done. Nor could you, with good judgment, select any one of them as a model for, say, a son of yours to follow. The richer of them might give you momentary pause as you thought of his possessions and influence, but not, I am sure, when you knew what he went through, and what he did to get them, and what he goes through and has to do today to hold on to them.

Indeed, it is doubtful if you would feel at ease in the vicinity of any one of them, even though they had on their most becoming clothes and their most engaging manners, and were especially attentive to you. Something about them, you would have found, was jarring something within you. At first you might not have understood just what this was, although you felt it keenly. But had you been using those highly sensitive, penetrating, X-raylike perceptive faculties of yours as you should have been, you would have known what it was instantly. For then you would have mentally seen into their interiors and have discovered that the thoughts they were throwing off had come into contact with your own thoughts, and that the two thought streams were so at variance as to be causing friction.

In spite of their outward show of personal importance, all three of our exhibits, you would have found, were quite ordinary specimens of the *genus homo,* each with virtually the same characteristics, habits, routines, limitations, and errors as the other two. And of all their flaws and faults, you would probably have decided after giving them a thorough going-over, the most damaging, not only to themselves but to the world in which they lived, was the wide discrepancy between what each of them was pretending to be and to do on the outside and what each of them was actually up to on the inside, in among his supposedly secret and hidden ambitions, desires, intentions, longings, lusts, and covetings.

Mentally exploring into this contrariety of theirs to find, if possible, a satisfying reason for it, will provide you with no end of interesting fact-finding adventure. And not merely in connection with our three exhibits, but because this particularly corrupting defection in inner attitude and outward

[111]

practice has become so common among human beings and is so little checked and corrected that it has become, all the experts agree, the most consistent winner in the hit parade of major human errors. Which makes abundantly clear, of course, why it is that of all the forms of life on earth we humans happen to be virtually the only ones that attempt the impossible feat of trying to maintain existence on a system of duality—that is, of being one thing outside, something else inside—and hoodwinking ourselves into believing that we are getting away with it.

All of which, you will quite easily see, makes these three friends of mine—and remember we are using them as scapegoats for all our sins of omission and commission—the only double-faced . . . double-minded . . . double-hearted . . . double-talking . . . double-acting . . . double-dealing creatures either in or out of captivity. (Isn't it a relief to get all those sins off our heads and onto theirs!) And that is the type of human being, you will remember, that that superlative prophet and teacher—Jesus of Nazareth—so directly thundered at, as he warned humanity against divided kingdoms that always come to desolation, and "cities and towns divided against themselves, which shall not stand."

[112]

It has already been agreed that our three human exhibits are about as dead as they ever will be. True, they exhibit a certain amount of biological animation, but to estimate correctly any man's aliveness one must go far beyond mere physicality, which is but a passing effect, and take account of his more important mental, spiritual, moral, and social development, and just what he has done and is doing to make the world less difficult for others. On this broad and only reliable scale of measurement their degree of aliveness is very low indeed, for not one of them is using more than a mere fraction of his capacities, his talents, and his abilities; and, most regrettable of all, each is using even this fraction in the wrong direction.

As a physical specimen each of them is a good insurance risk. As integers in population, political affairs, and the war effort, in which mobs of animated human bodies are needed, each of them has a value of being one more. In their orbits of daily living, where boundaries are narrow and self predominates, each of them flourishes in the way he likes best. But as citizens of the universe, wherein each is for all and all for each, they are unconditioned flops, fiascos, fizzles, and failures. This may seem like an uncharitable thing to say about them, but remember they are scapegoats, and it is up to us to dump all we can onto their heads before we turn them loose again in their own private wildernesses.

What had plunged these scapegoats into the relatively low state of humanity in which they exist at present would have been apparent to you from the very start of the exhibition if your mental eyes had been sharp. Each of them, you would have detected, had virtually stopped thinking and was drifting around with the currents of other people's thoughts, of mass feelings, and of mass emotions. True, they were doing a certain amount of self-centered mental functioning, but very little individual, outgoing thinking. And, observing this, you would have found out, too, that in just the degree that they had shut down on their capacities for independent and universal thinking, they had stopped growing, expanding, developing, and so, being alive.

## Chapter Sixteen

## YOU AND *YOU!*

One of the particularly fascinating things about exploring from the seat of a rocking chair is that no matter how far you think out, or up, or down, or around, or even into new dimensions, you will meet YOURSELF all the way going out there, as well as all the way coming back. To the uninitiated this may sound like something coming through the barred windows of an insane asylum, but not so to those accustomed to exploring beyond their biological frontiers, for they know from personal experience that the meeting with one's larger SELF beyond the prisonlike confines of his little finite self is not only the most thrilling and satisfying of adventures, but at the same time a fulfilling of one's cosmic obligation to FIND HIMSELF . . . KNOW HIMSELF . . . BE HIMSELF . . . and SHARE HIMSELF.

"But isn't sitting in a rocking chair doing nothing but thinking merely a lazy man's way of avoiding having to do something practical in a world of stern reality and facts?" you may mentally ask at this point, aiming a beam of suspicion in what would be my physical direction, if you knew how and where to localize me. "Do you mean to say that anyone can get ahead in this difficult and effortful experience of Life, by idly rocking back and forth in a chair, daydreaming, or dabbling with that metaphysical stuff?"

To which I will want to reply: "Thanks a lot for thinking those questions just then, for they enable me to tee up the whole idea in an exposed position, so that you can either pick it up and use it to your personal advantage, or boot it into oblivion, where, I am sure you will agree with me, all unprovable things have to land sooner or later, and the sooner the better.

In order to accomplish this program in an effective way, I should like to wave my invisible magic wand in a certain secret manner known only to a few, and conjure up a great array of colored floodlights and spotlights, and with them the largest and most powerful public-address amplifier obtainable. Then over the latter I should have announced a very special presentation, the presentation of one of the most important, indispensable, and unique individuals in all the world, and in the breathtaking pause that followed, introduce You, with lights, the blare of trumpets, and everything!

There's no catch in this, I assure you, or any

least trace of sarcasm, or any double meaning, or any comedy-comebacks, or any insincerity. I mean it! You ARE one of the most important, indispensable, and unique individuals in all the world, even in all the universe. That I will underwrite. And I will underwrite it regardless of any rating you may have given yourself, or accepted for yourself, in the ever-changing scale of human values. And the more you mentally adventure outside that little physical, finite you into the real and boundless dimensions of the real You, which of course can only be done mentally and spiritually, the more you will find this to be true.

Now if you will retire for a brief time into that part of your mind where you gossip with yourself about yourself, and where you do your private planning and plotting, as well as your private wondering and worrying, you will find that deep in there you have always had the feeling, if not the actual conviction, that you are lots better and lots more important than you appear to be outwardly; and that you are entitled to lots more fun, happiness, and success than you are getting out of your everyday existence. Well, the straight fact of the matter, my Hearty, is that you were abso· lutely correct about these feelings and convictions! You ARE lots better and more important than you appear to be, and you ARE entitled to lots

[117]

more fun, happiness, and success than you are now getting out of existence.

You don't have to take my word for this, though, for, if you will but continue exploring around within those amazing mental areas of yours, you will be able to find how true it is by yourself. And not only that, but you will learn in these personal explorations that this feeling or conviction about greater possibilities and accomplishments for yourself, with its almost invariable accompanying longing to escape . . . to expand . . . to be better . . . to do better . . . to have more . . . and to do more . . . is emanating from the divine fact of your past, present, and forever spiritually mental perfection. And that all of it is emanating, not from you as you, as you may have believed, but from the great primal Cause, Energy, and All-Presence, which most people reverently call God.

As you mentally continue in these explorations, finding and following individual clews in a spirit of high adventure and at your particular rate of progress or unfoldment, you will discover another great and reassuring fact. This: that the radiant, life-giving, space-filling Perfection, of which you should be getting clearer views through the fogs and mists of your physical senses, has never been interrupted and never can be interrupted, except through the illusive distortions of an unreal sense

[118]

of things, like looking at a beautiful landscape through glasses not properly adjusted to your eyes, and seeing everything distorted, and the distortions magnified.

The recovery of this original state of Perfection is usually regarded as the greatest goal of all adventures, of all exploring. And the greatness of it lies in the tremendous but simple fact that YOU ARE THE ADVENTURE! It begins in You! It is contained in You! It continues in You! It never gets outside You! For the adventure is You! When once you really get your mental fingers on this, your days and nights can never be dull, discouraging, or unproductive again. But while all adventure—and, of course, the exploring —has to begin in You, it never ends there. For real Life, and that means your individual expression of It is eternal. All the outstanding spiritual thinkers agree on that point. Agree too that because of the perfection of this all-embracing, eternally functioning, vitalizing, living Presence, there can be no reality whatsoever to such phenomena as decay, death, separation, the tragedy of being forgotten and all the other ills of human experience, regardless of all human opinions to the contrary.

To get off the main highway of thinking about these things and make a few shortcuts, let's pretend that, following a tip from me, you have placed that physical body of yours in a rocking chair, and are about to take off on a reconnaissance flight into the unknown back country of your own mind. Please note, even though we are only pretending, that you were asked to "place" your body in the chair, not to get into it. This distinction is most important in aiding one to get out of self and into SELF. Always put your body into a chair, never get into it. By the same token, try putting your body in bed, instead of going to bed; giving your body a bath, instead of taking a bath; feeding your body, instead of having meals; taking your body downtown with you, instead of going downtown. You will be most agreeably surprised at what this will do for you!

As the physical part of you rocks back and forth and the mental part of you moves out in the best direction you know from moment to moment, you will sooner or later make the revealing discovery that what you are actually moving toward is that great goal of attainment promised in the first chapter of Genesis, wherein God created all things, saw that they were "very good," and then gave man dominion over them. A dominion that never has been and never can be taken from him, according to advanced thinkers, because of the inseparable relation between Creator, created, and creation.

## Chapter Seventeen

## PRACTICE FLIGHT

As as result of our adventuring thus far, I am going to assume three things about you at this point. The first: that, thanks to the real meaning back of those fingerprints of yours, and in spite of so much think-alikeness, look-alikeness, and act-alikeness among the members of the human species, you now understand in a more workable way the importance of yourself as an individual entity, and that, as such, you have something individual and distinctly your own to give to the world that no one else can possibly give. The second: that you see more clearly than you did before that your mental and spiritual individuality is the real You, the infinite expression of an infinitely divine Cause, and that your finite personality is a temporary physical appearance, or mask, that tends to conceal the real You from you. And the third: that this precious heritage of individuality is to be accepted with gratitude and humility, cultivated to the utmost, and lived without compromise.

All genuine mental adventurers have these three

points firmly fixed in thought whenever they take off from their rocking chairs to explore and charter their own minds, or if you prefer, their worlds of awareness. To illustrate at least something of the technique of this kind of adventure, and to make it personal and intimate, let's make you the explorer in this particular instance and see what comes out of it. The first thing you will have to do is to find yourself a rocking chair for the enterprise. This is most important. Any old chair with a cushion in it and a roll to it will not do. It must have a chassis that complements yours and rockers under it that will match your moods of movement; otherwise you are handicapped right from the beginning. For always remember that a good rocking chair is just as essential to a mental and spiritual pilot as a good plane is to an air pilot.

But while the chair is important in its role of being a definite type of furniture for supporting your physical body and keeping it in pleasing motion, it is even more valuable to you as a symbol. Viewed from this angle, the chair becomes a living companion, teacher, and guide; and in its symbolism an eloquent expression of such longed-for things as peace . . . tranquillity . . . encouragement . . . reassurance . . . co-ordination . . . rhythm . . . harmony . . . grace . . . ease of movement . . . progress . . . revelation . . . and attainment.

[122]

Having found the right chair, you will then have
to find a fitting place for it, which can be an adventure by itself in these days of human gregarious-
ness, confusion, and noise. But having found the
right place, you loosen your body as much as possible, slump it into the chair, and set them both in
motion at a slow tempo. Then you deepen your
breathing until it is in rhythm with the motion
of the chair and your body. Your purpose in this
is to bring all of you into as perfect co-ordination
as possible, then to integrate this with the rhythm
of the chair, and then to blend mind, body, and
chair with the great rhythms of the universe.

In this effort, provided you go about it correctly,
you suddenly find a definite and most interesting
evaporating process happening to your physical
body, or rather, to the concept you have of that
body: a concept you may have been allowing more
or less to fill the foreground of your consciousness,
absorb practically all your attention, and blot out
most of the universe as far as you are concerned.
As you take the blinkers and blinders off your
thoughts and let them zoom up to where they
belong, you begin to observe that that human body
of yours is becoming less demanding, less trouble-
some, and less important. Then, like a motion
picture camera's fadeout, your body and all the
problems connected with it begin receding into

[123]

the background of your consciousness, until they disappear entirely and you become just your thinking; or in other words, you become an individual idea, capable of moving anywhere without restrictions of any kind.

You will not find achieving this state of mental and spiritual buoyancy easy at first, because of the whirling pressure of material-physical-human things in general, and those pivoting around your personality and private affairs in particular. All these material-physical-human objects, you will learn in one way or another, have to be eliminated before you start, in order that you may reach the mental altitude necessary for ventures of this kind. The old-time rocking-chairists describe this procedure as "heaving out the sandbags before taking off," meaning by that hypothetical sandbags filled with earthly thinking, which, they say, always keeps one heavy, saggy, dull, unresponsive to higher things, and fastened to the earth levels.

You will always know when the exact moment arrives for the mental take-off by the inner glow you feel, a glow invariably accompanied by an irresistible desire to be up and doing something-or-other to, or with, or about something-or-other. The temptation at this point will be for you to catapult your physical body into immediate action in order to satisfy that urge. But, being a good

[124]

rocking-chairist in the making, you will keep your body in the background, and first set your thinking into outward motion toward your fullest circumference. This pressure, as has already been pointed out, is caused by Explorer's Itch, resulting from the friction of thinking and living in margins too narrow and shallow for one, and inciting him to get out of them and enlarge the borders of his being . . . his seeing . . . his knowing . . . and his doing. Or else!

At this moment of effervescing, even of near internal combustion, you do a "thumbs-up!" Elevating them to where you can see distinctly those precious coat-of-arms prints on the face of them. This to remind you again of your cosmic individuality, of your cosmic importance, and of the cosmic need for you. And because of this importance, of the demand upon you to be your own individual self in everything you think, in everything you say, and in everything you do. When you have sufficiently impressed this individuality upon yourself, which by the way is a private consecration and dedication ceremony that every real rocking-chair explorer observes with himself, you swing one of those thumbs past the end of your nose in an outward direction and mentally follow along its wake.

As your thoughts leave their conventional

round-and-round pattern and begin to spiral, rising about your physical body, the rocking chair, the room in which they are, above the house, the city, the state, the nation, and even the earth itself, you should make a discovery that ought to fill you with no end of astonishment and amusement. This: that quite unconsciously and with almost no effort on your part, you are performing the remarkable feat of both sitting in a rocking chair and not sitting in it, at one and the same time. For, looking down from those high altitudes where you are mentally cruising, you will see with both wonder and delight that while the seen, or physical, part of you is rocking back and forth in that chair, the unseen, mental and spiritual part of you is moving around with the utmost freedom at enormous distances from them, and getting along very well without them, too. As the significance of this separation begins to dawn upon you, you should experience a fullness of being and a liberty of action you have never known before, and in that fullness and liberty, should know that you are definitely on your way to find the right answers to all things throughout the universe that need answers.

Rocking out physically, mentally, and spiritually in this way, you rock yourself into contact with "the great Cosmic Spirit, which sets the currents of Life in action." Then to the best of your abil-

[126]

ity you blend the allness of you into the Allness of It, keeping ever mentally alert, flexible, adaptable, receptive, and co-operative, but always individual in that co-operation. There is never any struggling necessary in this delectable adventuring, just a simple, natural, easy flowing along with Life as one's individual and essential part of It. And as you move along in this way, being as much of your complete self as you know how to be, you become a front-row aisle-seat witness, so to speak, of how good Life really is . . . how superbly Life has been planned . . . and how magnificently Life is being sustained and managed by what the American Indian reverently calls "THE BIG HOLY!"

## Chapter Eighteen

## MEET "A BIGGIE!"

Few experiences in living are likely to turn one into a confirmed mental and spiritual explorer more quickly than the discovery that his identity and existence extend incalculably beyond the bounds of his human body as well as the number of days supposedly allotted to him on earth. He may long have hoped that this other life were true, and he may have believed it in a hazy, theoretical sort of way, wishing, as he did so, that he could prove it for himself or see someone else demonstrate it. Then, as usually happens, while he is reading an inspired book, talking with a truly inspired man or woman, walking alone in an atmosphere of surpassing beauty, or perhaps sitting in silence, listening to things beyond the silence, there is a sudden flash of inner revelation, and he knows it to be true, knows it without the shadow of a doubt.

It is always a rib-spreading discovery, not alone because of the comfort it imparts, but for the opportunities it affords for individual exploration, individual expansion, and individual accomplishment. It provides the kind of adventuring wherein one gets a clearer understanding of what the great thinkers are really driving at when they say that Life was, is, and always will be a spiritually mental, unlimited, and eternal process; a process entirely independent of anything and everything having to do with the physical, the material, and the human. It provides the kind of adventuring too wherein one learns in the most direct of ways that the perfectly functioning state of existence that the ancients spoke of as "the Kingdom of Heaven" is not something distant and future, or something one has to die and be resurrected into, but a purified and spiritualized state of consciousness that all are equipped and privileged to think their way into whenever they care to make the effort.

Just how much of the beautiful, good, and true you have been missing in everyday experience by mistaking that skin-and-bone body of yours for You would be difficult to estimate correctly. But unless you are a very exceptional individual and so toweringly high above the average level of humanity, the answer is "Plenty"! This is not a private guess of my own, but the composite opinion of some of the world's best authorities on matters of this kind. And they, speaking from mellowed knowledge and long experience, say that because of our ingrowing and stubborn habit of identifying ourselves with only a minor fraction of OURSELVES, we humans, taking us as a whole, are scarcely alive, even with all our bustle, din, and ballyhoo.

Instead of spreading ourselves to our true mental and spiritual proportions, and moving along with all Creation in the harmony and rhythm of Life and Love, say these sharp-eyed observers, we hypnotize ourselves and one another into believing that each of us is shut up within so many pounds of materiality. Doing a life sentence at hard labor inside a skin-prison. A prison built of nothing but unreal, delusive beliefs. A prison in which each of us has incarcerated his highest sense of himself. A prison in which each of us is not only the prisoner, but judge, prosecutor, warden, executioner, and board of pardons as well. And this darkened state of thinking, they insist, is directly responsible for what they term our shocking backwardness in finding out about OURSELVES, what we should have known, what we should have been enjoying and sharing centuries ago.

What you and I look like physically, the manner in which we clothe our bodies, and what others may say about us openly and whisper behind our backs, are usually regarded as of the utmost im-

[130]

portance in tabulating our worth as individuals. On this basis human beings have been grabbed, graded, and grouped, ever since public records have been kept. But to the real connoisseur in individual values, such surface indications have relatively little importance, no matter how polished and publicized, or how momentarily prominent and flourishing. The connoisseurs go about judging men in a different way.

If, for instance, they could get the pair of us under their scrutiny, they would not be particularly interested in our outwardness. Or in our material possessions, even though we had many. Or in whom we knew socially, or had a pull with. Or to what we belonged. Or in how impressively and successfully we strutted our personalities. They would be interested in our inwardness. For, being experts, they would know that the human being in the raw state is like an iceberg floating about at the mercy of every wind that blows and every current that moves, with only a very small part in view and all the rest hidden. And being wise men, they would insist upon inspecting and checking our invisible qualities.

They would insist upon probing deep into the mental part of us and sniffing the quality of our thoughts. They would virtually disregard our surfaces, our possessions, our material accomplishments, and even our interpretations of ourselves; they would X-ray deep into our middles to see what we were really up to in our supposedly secret inner chambers, what we were plotting and planning with our motives, our inclinations, desires, lusts, longings, wishes, and ambitions. Which is the equivalent of saying that they would be more interested in the YOU of you and the ME of me, than in the you of YOU and the me of ME. For they would have known from long experience with specimens like us that only in the mental and spiritual can man be correctly evaluated as MAN.

To make this scrutiny a bit more realistic, and at the same time to head you in the direction of some soul-expanding adventure, let me make a suggestion. Tonight if it's clear overhead and the climate is right for it, slip out of doors without telling anyone your purpose, and take your body along with you. Then find a place that provides a panoramic view. The roof of your house will do admirably. Or the top of a mountain. Or a stretch of unfrequented beach. Or a real spread of desert. Or just a plain, friendly, back-country meadow. You will know when you reach the right spot, for your intuition, or, as the American Indian puts it, your in-knowing, will tell you.

Then spread your body flat, front upward, or lean it against something comfortable; next make all of you as still as you possibly can, and turn your eyes and thoughts skyward. You will not have the swing of a rocking chair to help you with this adventure, but that doesn't matter, for, if you are sensitive and receptive to what is going on, you will gradually become more and more aware that everything everywhere is moving, not only according to perfect law and order, but in perfect harmony and rhythm; and that mentally, at least, you are part of that movement. As you become conscious of this great fact, remind yourself again and again that your only responsibility is to let things happen. Don't try to drive your thoughts, or to lead them, or to herd them. Turn them loose and let them go where they please without any prodding from you. They'll come home to you again, and they'll come home bringing more than their tails behind them, too.

As you watch that lavish performance going on above you, and around you, and through you, that the greatest of all SHOWMEN puts on nightly for those who care to attend, you will, of course, be profoundly impressed. One could scarcely look into a night sky and not be impressed. But you will be taking in far more than an impression; you will be observing minutely the magnitude . . . the intricacies . . . the unity . . . the mathematical accuracy . . . the perfection . . . the beauty . . . the grandeur . . . and the smooth-working altogetherness of it all.

Then by a natural sequence it should dawn upon you, if it hasn't done so already, that you are not merely a spectator at this glittering pageant, but actually a performer in it yourself. From here on you will find yourself involved in the most superlative adventure. From one way of looking at it, you will be mentally heading out toward fascinating new horizons, moving away from that little finite you, and into the boundlessness of the infinite You; away from man and into MAN; and discovering more of YOURSELF all along the way. From another way of looking at it, you will be a spectator watching Life, appearing to you as your own Universe, reveal itself to you; your part in it being to keep fragrant, flexible, humble, and receptive; to look, to listen, and to feel with your whole being; and to let impressions sing through you as though they were the wind and you, an Aeolian harp.

As you move out more and more into the splendor of it all, or, if you prefer it said the other way around, as the splendor of it all moves through you and You, you and You may well exclaim with all the enthusiasm and vigor at your command: "What a performance the Author, Producer, and Director of all things is putting on tonight! What

[134]

flawless continuity! What immensity and super-excellence of accomplishment! And yet, nothing about the whole display, or in the whole display, is any more amazing in achievement than the stupendous fact that I am capable of spreading out my thinking, this consciousness of mine, and wrapping it around the whole show—earth, moon, stars, and everything!

"Not a single thing anywhere that I can identify is detached from me! Or unrelated to me! All that I see up there, or over yonder, or here about me, is not going on outside of me at all! It is all taking place within the borders of this astonishing mind of mine, and nowhere else! Were it taking place outside my mind, how could I possibly know anything about it? I couldn't, of course! All of which makes it clearly apparent that I include my Universe! That I have it inside me! It's all in and part of my mind . . . my consciousness . . . my subjective state of being . . . my personal thinking areas . . . my world of awareness! It's in and part of ME! It is ME! What I am really doing is looking at MYSELF! Enjoying MYSELF!"

And meeting YOURSELF thus, in the ever-enlarging mental and spiritual spread of YOU, would bring you face to face, so to speak, with "A Biggie," far beyond the most super-colossal meaning of that Hollywoodish term.

[135]

*Chapter Nineteen*

## DILEMMA

If you are planning to duck away from the congestion and pressure of human experience for a while, and for the first time solo out, rocking chair or otherwise, to penetrate into the hinterland of your mind, in order to discover if possible what You are really like, out there beyond yourself in the boundless stretches of YOURSELF, you are going to create some great character and history, even if you do only fairly well at the exploring. But as one adventurer to another, let me warn you that you are going to run into a major dilemma right at the start. A dilemma that is likely not only to befog, befool, and befuddle you, but to defy your best intellectual efforts either to explain it satisfactorily or to brush it off in the conventional manner.

It is one of those tricky, intimate dilemmas that has been bothering and baffling the members of the human species for a very long time. In fact, ever since those unprecedented days in the Garden of Eden when, as the celebrated tale goes, one of

Adam's ribs suddenly and most mysteriously disappeared from his skeleton while he slept, and with even more extraordinary suddenness and mystery, blossomed into a full-grown woman—named Eve. Following this miracle, you will recall, she became Adam's wife, without benefit of clergy. And then they became the first poppa and momma, as well as the grandparents of the human species, up to and including you and me. At least that is how the old tale goes, and a great tale it is, too, considering its ingredients and the length of time it has managed to keep in circulation against brilliant and stiff competition. But it is a tale, say those uncompromising experts in distinguishing between fact and fiction, the believing of which has been responsible for most of man's inability down through the ages to understand Life, the Universe, or Himself aright.

Starting out to explore YOURSELF, not yourself, remember, in order to live up to the individual, mandatory, cosmic obligation to FIND THYSELF . . . KNOW THYSELF . . . BE THYSELF . . . and SHARE THYSELF, you will find this dilemma rotating around that personal contrivance of head, arms, torso, and contents of yours. That object which you had to prod out of bed this morning, bathe, dress, feed, and then lug around with you wherever you went, so that the other human beings you met, with their

[137]

low visibility and limited understanding, could know that you were present.

In all rocking-chair adventuring, as has already been explained but is worth giving another flip to, the procedure is simple, and its possibilities more promising of good for you than anything you have been able to dream to date. You merely park your body in the chair you like, set them both in motion, and then in your own individual way, and strictly following your own leads, think outwardly and upwardly as far as you can. But be sure as you do this that you keep mentally flexible and alert, and in that alertness, that you observe and listen attentively to everything that appears within the range of your awareness, remembering always that while you have something distinctly your own to share with everything everywhere, everything everywhere has something distinctly its own to share with you. For that's how creation has to function to keep going in the brilliant and successful way it does.

In these journeyings, let it be repeated again, your human body will be of no use to you at all. In fact, it will only be in your way. For the regions you will explore are the physically unseeable, spiritually mental environment, or universe, spreading itself to unguessable distances in every direction all about you. Or, to state it with more

[138]

scientific correctness, within You. The only environment, or universe, by the way, in which, according to the most reliable authorities, anyone
will ever be able to find that enduring good for
which all of us, either directly or indirectly, are so
eagerly seeking.

Human bodies, even in their most perfect ap-
pearances and functions, have ever been humanity's most pressing concern, as you no doubt are
very well aware. Also the cause of its most
chronic philosophical and moral headaches. And
all of them due to the highly involved, embarrassing problems connected with bodies. Problems,
for instance, arising from the glaring faults of design and construction in the bodies themselves.
Problems of maintenance, of trying to keep them
alive, in good working order, and up to the prevailing anatomical and social standards. And very
particularly, problems concerned with trying to
manage them successfully, according to the current ethical rules and one's private conscience.

To turn all of this into more of an adventure
for you, let me again suggest this: toss your human
body, but gently of course, into a rocking chair,
forget it, take the top off that conventional coop
in which you crowd your thoughts, and let them
scatter! Don't try to direct them. Don't even
be responsible for them. Give them their com-

plete freedom for a change. Don't even advise
them as to what you wish or expect them to bring
back to you. Let them attend to that. Don't
worry, you'll be well rewarded if you do your part
correctly. And you will be rewarded, because in
that simple gesture of letting go you will have
reversed the human futility of trying to explain
creation from a limited, finite sense of things, and
have given creation an opportunity to reveal ITS
meaning and purpose to you in ITS own way.

On this all-out exploring into the uncharted
back country of YOU, you will come upon two facts
that are going to be of enormous importance to
you in everything you do from here on. Facts
you will want to remind yourself of again and
again. Facts with which every rocking-chair explorer begins his adventures. Facts that can re-
move every barrier and handicap from your
personal experience. Facts that can give you freedom and attainment beyond your fondest expecta-
tions. They have been mentioned before, but are
worth much repetition. The first of these is the
enormous distance to which you can spread your
thinking. And the second, the almost incredible
number, size, and variety of things you are *so* easily
able to contain within your thinking, that is,
within YOU.

As you mentally expand yourself to these far-out proportions, give some real thought, your own thought, not that of others, to just what all this means to you as an individual living entity in the plan and purpose of creation. Your conventional academic training and human intellect may not be of much service to you in this, because of their definite limitations. But a divinely motivated, ever-revealing Something, call it what you wish, can and will help you, and most magnificently, provided you are sufficiently humble and receptive. And with this potent co-operation, which you should find as intimately related to you and as natural as your breathing, you will be on your merry and adventurous way toward removing from your path everything that even remotely threatens your freedom, harmony, and on-going success.

Then, by way of a dramatically grand anti-climax, contract the vast beamspread of that thinking of yours, throw it into reverse, and aim its bright but narrow focus on your human body, which you are supposed to have left parked in a rocking chair. Study that body for a while in an impersonal way, and then as part of the adventure; try to compute the amount of time in years, months, weeks, days, and hours you have devoted to it. To such efforts, for instance, as trying to keep the thing alive and functioning comfortably . . . to keeping it socially presentable . . . to

[141]

stuffing food, pouring various kinds of liquids, and inhaling smoke into it . . . to trying to impress or attract others with it . . . to admiring and indulging it . . . to daydreaming, bragging, and worrying about it. You'll be surprised! You may even be shocked and embarrassed!

Having these human bodies of ours, and it is your privilege to find out why you have yours and why it looks and behaves as it does, we are all inherently ambitious to keep them at a maximum of perfection. We want them to be sound and healthy. We want them to be attractive, even alluring. We want them to be enduring and useful. But except for relatively brief periods of time, our bodies, or something-or-other connected with them, "cross us up" (to borrow a bit of modern language). In this crossing up our bodies, in spite of our best efforts to prevent it, go through a harrowing process of losing their vigor, shape, and style; become old, saggy, useless, and unattractive; and then as a climax to the depressing routine, die, decay, and disappear.

Just what happens to the person who owns the body and is supposed to be living inside the thing when it disappears in this fashion is, for most people, the most confusing and distressing part of the whole dilemma. And what makes it so particularly confusing and distressing is that it is one of those bitter and unavoidable riddles of existence that sooner or later each of us has to face alone and solve alone. And our success in facing and solving the riddle, according to the most reliable authorities, depends entirely on just how much reality each of us believes there is in the material-physical-human sense of existence that seems to be going on all about us, and of which each of us seems to be such a certain, but at the same time uncertain, part.

## Chapter Twenty

## IN-AND-OUTER

Once, while wandering around in the Orient, trying to satisfy an insatiable but friendly curiosity to know at first hand just what it is that makes all things tick the way they do, I came upon a picturesque individual who is not only worth sharing, but who in a way aptly illustrates the chronic dilemma of the human body. He was a kindly faced, bronze-colored, skinny little "holy man." And I found him just where I should have discovered him, sitting cross-legged on top of a hill that commanded sweeping views in all directions, looking off into, and I know far beyond, a gorgeous saffron sunset. That I disturbed his solitude and meditations didn't seem to bother him in the least, and his smile was so gracious that I couldn't resist joining him.

Getting an invisible bridge set up between us, so that I could mentally go over into him and he could come over into me, in that ever-stimulating and expanding unity of relationships, was easy.

[144]

Then we talked freely and I began finding out things about him. For a long time, I learned, he had been on a continuous pilgrimage, ever seeking greater spiritual enlightenment and always looking for the God-essence in everything, no matter how lowly and seemingly insignificant. His wanderings had taken him far and wide. He had no scheduled plan for them; he just up and went whenever the promptings came. Sometimes these impulses sent him into almost inaccessible mountain solitudes, sometimes into crowded cities, sometimes just following the road. Whenever his spiritual indicator was low, he sought and then sat at the feet of some teacher; when it was in the upper levels, he shared what he had with others.

His worldly possessions consisted of a loincloth, a much-mended old cloak, a few toilet articles, and two sacred books. But this lack of goods was more than made up for by his inner opulence. Like all the rest of us, he was both consciously and unconsciously carving new facets of HIMSELF into human visibility. Some of these he had chipped and polished to such a high degree of transparency that his God-being shone through with both splendor and warmth. Other facets of HIMSELF, facets that the average Occidental, with his stress on the material, rates so highly, he had never even attempted to do any work on. But this

[145]

can be said of him, his average in being was high, but no higher than the courage he had in daring to live his own life in his own way.

Seldom have I encountered such spontaneous, unselfish goodness as that little fellow possessed. He didn't talk about it; it oozed out of him in everything he said and did. He always looked for the expression of the Divine in every human, animal, snake, insect, bird, or inanimate thing he met, and always saluted it mentally if not always vocally. With but one exception, as far as I could observe, he loved everything. That one exception was his human body. It wasn't much of a body as bodies go; it couldn't have been, with the lack of care, the undernourishment, and the severe discipline it was getting from him. But he felt that such harsh treatment was necessary if he hoped to attain the high goal he had set for himself and toward which he was struggling with a heavy load of musts and must nots and a variegated assortment of private punishments.

He had been in close association with that body of his for a long time, with unlimited opportunities for observing its every mood and movement, and for studying its every function. But in spite of all these opportunities, and all his meditating, he had never arrived at one original conclusion about that body. As a matter of fact—and please

[146]

understand that this is not said down my nose at
him from a supposedly superior point of view, because I have too much respect for him to do that
—his thoughts about his body were slogging
heavy-footedly round and round in a narrow, traditional circle, getting nowhere at all except back
to where they started from.  Like an elephant
clinging to the tail of the elephant ahead, and although full of well-meaning effort, doing a kind of
meaningless ring-around-the-rosy.

Through a little deft probing, I learned that
his human body had him almost completely
stymied.   It wasn't at all clear to him why he had
to have such a liability, with what he regarded as its
strange and unpredictable moods, its insubordi-
nations, and its unresponsiveness to the control he
tried to exercise over it.   And having his particular body, he was never quite sure what he ought to
do with it, especially in connection with his spiritual ambitions.   So he was treating it like an un-
wanted problem child that someone who wished
him no good at all had left on his back steps.   "I
don't know why you are here," he would, in substance, say to his body, "but as long as you are here,
and as long as I don't know what to do with you,
stay and serve God!   But remember, I'm keeping
both eyes on you!"

As we sat in the glow of that unforgettable sun-

[147]

set, swapping opinions and now and then a real idea, I did something that was equivalent to unpinning a hand grenade and tossing it into his lap. Without any warning at all I asked him whether he believed his body included him, or he included his body? That is, I hastened to add, was he as a living entity cooped up inside his human body, in there with an assortment of organs and other things with which to keep it alive and a private mind with which to think it around? Or was his body merely a shadow-shape, ghosting around inside his own mind, or consciousness, projected by himself, and so entirely subject to what he thought about it?

Up to that moment, his answers had been as spontaneous, as fluid, and as frank as a child's, but when I pulled that one out from nowhere, he went into what a vaudeville performer would have called "a dead-pan silence." He distinctly heard the words I used, and he knew what they meant, but not in the sequence in which I had so suddenly marched them. I waited for some little time, and then went at it again with all sorts of variations in words and gestures. But the essence of it was the same: was he, actually speaking, living inside his body, or living outside it? If inside it, how and why? And if outside it, how and why, too? It was plain that no one had ever asked him such a question before. It was equally plain, too, that he had never asked it of himself.

I could almost hear his mental gears meshing and unmeshing, even grinding, as he strained for an opinion, for a quotation, for anything in fact with which to meet the emergency. But none came. Gradually the far-reaching import of the question began dawning on him. His face plainly indicated that. Then he spoke, slowly, and with a tone of deep solemnity. The question, he said, was a difficult one and would require much study and meditation. Was he inside his body, or his body inside him? He muttered the question a few times to himself, then lapsed again into that dead-pan silence, his body becoming as motionless as the tree under which we sat. The physical part of him was there all right, but where the rest of him had gone I couldn't have guessed. He was searching, I knew, for a satisfying answer to one of humanity's most ancient and baffling riddles.

At long last the rest of him returned to where he had left his body, fetching back with him what obviously was the best conclusion he was able to find either going out or coming back. It took him some minutes to make it vocal, owing to the care with which he had to select his words and set them in sequence. The question, he told me, was unusually difficult, because it was so involved in mystery, and so could be answered correctly only by those who had great illumination. His personal belief about the matter, however—subject, of course, to change as greater wisdom came—was that he lived inside his body, except when he meditated or slept, at which time, he confided to me, he left his body and enjoyed the utmost freedom of movement and accomplishment. But just how he managed to get in and out of that skin-casing of his with such flawless facility was beyond his comprehension. It just happened like that, he said, he didn't know how, and perhaps he wasn't supposed to know.

*Chapter Twenty-one*

## OLD GOOSEBERRY

It should be apparent to anyone capable of poking his mental periscope above the fogs generated by his physical senses and having a look around that no one is going to get very far in understanding the real meaning of Life, and what is expected of him in It, until he first solves the ancient riddle of his human body, the same riddle that so completely baffled the skinny little holy man mentioned in the last chapter. And what makes the riddle such a seemingly tough one to crack, say the experts, is not so much the problem in itself, but the attitude of those trying to solve it. An attitude, they point out, compounded of faulty education, organized ignorance, and the reluctance of the average human being to do his own thinking except under the pressure of necessity, except when the blowtorch of Old Man Fate is scorchingly close to his individual experience.

What makes this attitude so pertinent at the moment is that we are in the midst of one of those blowtorch periods right now. And in a most wholesale and blistering way, too, as you must have observed for yourself as you took in current history through the newspapers, the radio, your private-information grapevine, and the things you may have been seeing and going through. If you have been reacting to these events in the manner common to most people, what you have read, heard, seen, and otherwise sensed has not only disturbed you deeply, but filled you with grave alarm for your loved ones as well as for yourself. Suddenly, but with plenty of warning, we were all flung up against something grim, relentless, diabolical, and utterly horrible. Something with which relatively few know how to cope. It is the shocking rate at which human bodies are disappearing from the human scene in the phenomenon of death. The phenomenon of so-called natural death, of accidental death, of privately inflicted death, but, most appalling of all, of death by wholesale slaughter and by wholesale starvation.

Like riding down a fantastic, international shoot-the-chutes, we were all precipitated into the most unrestrained and incredible lunatic stampede in all history. A mental, moral, and physical stampede of such revolting proportions as to have already established a new all-time low in human depravity. A stampede record in ruthlessness and destruction and premeditated evil that no jungle animal could possibly equal. That in itself was bad enough, but added to it were the dismal predictions by the professional observers of what lay ahead for our boasted civilization and for each one of us in particular; and on top of that, the atmospheric pressure we all began to feel in varying degrees from the lonely, sobbing cry of "WHY?" surging out in bitter anguish from the crushed minds and hearts of so many millions upon millions of men, women, and children.

All of which, quite naturally, is having an unprecedented revolutionizing effect on the thinking and living of every human being riding the earth. Our tottering civilization, as the professional observers describe it, the tumult and terror of the times, and the fear-driven effort to save one's own hide are forcing each of us, in one way or another, to make some kind of an effort to do his own thinking or exploring, whether he wants to or not. It's the blowtorch of Old Man Fate at our individual and collective tails! And when one feels that he has little desire left to linger along the way. These are days in which the material-physical-human props are failing as never before. Days in which everyone is being forced to re-examine, to test, and to reassort his subjective and objective values. Days in which each one of us is having to learn that he must either think out as an individual into his real being and share himself fully in this capacity, or feel that afflictive blowtorch until he does.

But whether one becomes a mental explorer by choice or pressure, the moment he does so he finds himself up against that inevitable riddle of the human body. It may be the riddle of human bodies in general. It could be the riddle of his own body, which may have become diseased, injured, devitalized by bad habits, or burdensome with age. Or it might be the riddle of the body of a loved one, which has disappeared from human visibility, leaving him lonely and desolate. But lying back of all of them is the controlling key-riddle of whether, as living entities, we are inside our bodies, or our bodies inside us—that is, inside our minds or thinking areas.

If, as so many believe, without doing much original thinking about it one way or another, we are living inside our bodies and so are subject to their whims, moods, feelings, averages of chance, mutability, and disappearance, then the outlook ahead is hopeless for all of us. But, on the contrary—and this belief is what all seasoned mental explorers subscribe to—if we are outside these bodies of ours, and the bodies merely "such stuff as dreams are made on"—that is, shadow things of our own fancy, and so subject to our own fancy—

[154]

then all is exceedingly well with all of us, whether we seem to be "here" or "dead"; and this, mind you, regardless of what our material senses may be screaming to the contrary.

Whoever it was that first felt himself qualified to clear his throat and then formally hand down to his fellow beings the decision that they lived inside their human bodies, and that when these bodies died and came to an end, the occupants of them died and came to an end too, will never be known because he lived too far back in antiquity. But what he started, either as a conviction or a hoax, has certainly had freewheeling down through the centuries. Here and there clear-visioned, stouthearted nonconformists have risen in advanced foxholes and let drive with everything they have, in a valiant effort to deflate the ancient error and set mankind free from such mesmeric nonsense. But, in spite of all they have done, the old gooseberry—and anciently this term symbolized the devil, or a sinister force that played havoc—still rolls on, not so well as it did, to be sure, but still rolls.

If your experience runs according to the traditional pattern, you began to be impressed by this antiquated error at about the time you were being rated as "the cutest, most beautiful, and most wonderful baby in all the world." And the old gooseberry, which was ever thereafter to make you more and more body-conscious and so more and more restricted, was probably started rolling in your mental direction at about the point in your babyhood when you were just budding into self-consciousness, able to distinguish between a few objects, and, while awfully "umday anday oopidstay," smart enough to know how to use the sophisticated technique of noise and bluff for attracting special attention and service to yourself.

What most of us were taught to believe in those early days was that each of us had a private skin-and-bone body with which, whether we cared to do so or not, we had to navigate through a relatively brief, tempestuous, and uncertain existence as best we could and as well as others would permit us, with the odds heavily against us all the way. In addition to having this body, each of us was supposed to be living inside the thing. Supposed to be living in there with a messy-looking assortment of organs, a rather vaguely understood actuating essence known as a soul, and a muggy mass of stuff called a brain, with which we thought our bodies around and, they said, caused them to perform rational acts and be civilized.

Just why an intelligent Cause with good taste and friendly inclinations would want us, "superior expressions of intelligent life," to spend our time riding around inside such amateurishly designed, damp, overcrowded, badly ventilated, depressing quarters, when so much free and lovely space is available in the universe, was never made clear to us.    And this, I suspect, was due to the fact that so many of our teachers didn't know the reason themselves, but were merely handing along in the orthodox manner what someone else had told them. But there we were supposed to be, nevertheless, each of us cooped up in his private body, and each getting information about the world through two peepholes in the front of his head, and holes on either side that he used as listening posts.

Thus imprisoned within our skin-containers, according to the old gooseberry, each of us is supposed to be whirled and swirled through a maelstrom of existence over which he has virtually no control at all.    Like riding in a runaway rollercoaster!    Never certain whether the next propulsion will send us up or down, to right or to left, into something or out of something!    Or whether the next minute will bring us good or ill, happiness or unhappiness, success or failure, the beginning of great things or the end of everything!    Cynics often speak of this tossing about as the original form of being taken for a ride!    A ride, they lugubriously point out, in which no one has the slightest chance to escape his particularly arranged doom from the moment the finger is laid on him at birth until it is time for him to be rubbed out in death!

But remember, my Hearty, that an old gooseberry is an old gooseberry, no matter how long it has rolled, or how loudly it squeaks in the rolling!

*Chapter Twenty-two*

## DOUGHNUTS

One of the most effective steps toward solving the riddle of the human body and the swarms of lesser riddles accompanying it is to quit trying to find the right answers inside the body, or even on a mental level with it.   No one ever has been able to solve them in that way, and no one ever will be able to do so either.   And the reason for this?   The great metaphysical fact that regardless of how others may be picturing you, or you may be regarding yourself, you are, at this moment, a spiritually mental being of such prodigious proportions that you could no more be crammed within skin-dimensions than you could stuff your particular universe inside a sausage-casing.

This will become increasingly clearer as you pay more attention to the vast areas of your thinking capacities, and begin taking advantage of the opportunities they afford for expanding the range of your being.   Out as far as your imagination can go, out as far as that do you actually go as a living entity.   All that, and indescribably more, too, is your unseen unlimitable, ever-enduring, spiritually mental body. Or, if the phrase is easier for you to grasp, your embodiment. The embodiment of everything that you can identify, of everything that you know. The objects your physical senses seem to cognize as being out there, are not out there at all, you will come to discover, but inside your thinking, inside your consciousness, inside You. The only thing that can include You is the perfected ONENESS, the TOTALITY, and the ALLNESS of the GOD-PRESENCE Itself.

Consequently, you have never been inside that human body of yours, strange as that may appear! And what's more, you couldn't possibly get in there, even with the help of all the anatomical experts, magicians, and burglars in the world. You could disagree vehemently with this statement, of course, and insist that you are inside your body, that everyone knows you are, and that you could get affidavits to prove that you had been carrying on in there for years. But even if you called in an entire staff of skilled surgeons to help you prove it, and they went through you as only surgeons know how to go through a body, not one of them would be able to find the slightest trace of the real You. They would find a quantity of materiality in human form that you had been using to impress others, but not You.

You might be disappointed and embarrassed to find yourself evicted thus from your body, without having been inside it; but there would be compensations, for the experience would no doubt set you to thinking out in new directions. And the more you explored around in your far-outness, the more you would come to see that while your body is definitely yours, it most definitely is not You. And the more you gave consideration to this idea, the more clearly you would come to realize that your body is simply a concept, a concept of your own and other people's thinking, an unsubstantial shadow-appearance that You can think around, but that has neither power, ability, nor intelligence to think You around. In other words, you can think about it, but it cannot think about you.

While some of the foregoing observations have been repeated with variations in other chapters of this book, and are mentioned again for quite apparent reasons, none of them are my dicta. They are, rather, composite thoughts of some of the greatest mental and spiritual explorers down through the ages. Those rare ground-and-lofty adventurers have always been hunting for more of that Truth that was to set not only themselves but all mankind free. They are apostles of the impossible, always willing to take unusual chances to attain unusual ends. They are unmatchable spiritual individualists who, in a sadly massed-up and messed-up world of hypnotically controlled crowds, gangs, mobs, and multitudes, dare to live their own lives for the good of all, without compromise, and dare to encourage others to do just that too.

If you and I could look through the personality-exteriors, the words, and the deeds of these great men and women, and study the motives back of them, we would gain an enriching experience. For, in that intimate penetration, we would find almost flawless technique in letting real BEING, or GOD, function through one's identity, as one's identity. We would discover, too, in that intimate searching, how it is possible for them to go through the difficulties that beset them with such unwavering loftiness of purpose . . . such zeal for living . . . such fearlessness . . . such unselfishness . . . and to achieve such enduring results.

Their method is simple, but virtually futile when attempted halfheartedly or for selfish purposes. And here it is, reduced to its essence: having first conquered themselves by unselfing and purifying their motives, they are able to attain and travel at great mental and spiritual altitudes. From these sublimated elevations, high above the fogs and storms generated by centuries of wrong thinking, they are able, with their clear vision, to see through the forms, symbols, names, and beliefs of material-physical-human things, and make contact with the realities back of them. Are able to see through the seemingly solid phenomenal universe, to behold the real one in all its glory, and to find and be their eternally assigned but never static part, in its never-interrupted, harmonious functions.

And they accomplish this, it is most helpful to note, not through intellectual formulas, or hand-me-down, humanly prescribed procedure, but by means of that swift, photographic revelation that comes only through individual spiritual illumination.

There is no hocus-pocus about this. Nothing occult, or mysterious, or esoteric, or dangerous to monkey with, or even abstruse. To them, the coming of this revealing awareness of the ALL moving through the all, with perfection . . . harmony . . . rhythm . . . love . . . and steady purpose, is as natural as being a ray in the shining of the sun. But it is a relationship, and it is an experience, they caution, that can come only to the pure in heart—that is, to the pure in motives, intentions, desires, and such basic mental things.

With their profound knowledge, their love for mankind, but with a keen ability to see through pretense, falsehood, and the most subtle of deception, it is not difficult to understand why they are so free from illusions about the human being, either as a species or as an individual specimen. On this point they seem to be both undeceivable and unbluffable. But they reverse the usual order in these matters, and appraise the human inwardly instead of outwardly. They want to know what each human being is up to within the supposedly secret chambers of himself, and not so much about his physical appearance, what organizations he belongs to, whom he knows, how he earns his living, or what material things he possesses.

Penetrating into him in this denuding manner, and judging him not only impersonally but all the way down to his deepest mental depths, they know him, until individually reclaimed and refined, to be one of the most, if not the most, deceptive, treacherous, dangerous, and ruthless forms of predatory life moving about the earth. To which they add, and obviously from long and sharp experience, that while the human is to be helped in every wise way possible, it is most important while doing so, especially in periods of forced growth like the present, to keep him under close surveillance, like a partly tamed wild animal, until such time as he is able to recognize his innate divinity and be it.

[164]

According to these discriminating analysts, what makes everyday living so difficult and discouraging for most of us is our cultivated habit of just supposing things that are not true, and then trying to live, and to force others to live, as though they were. And of all these supposings, they insist, the most popular and handicapping is that one about the human body. The supposition spinning around the notion that each of us is a relatively unimportant little dab of existence, made up of highly perishable material elements, and stuffed inside a skin-carton. And that being thus impounded, we are anchored perpetually to a particular family, group, locality, occupation, race, nationality, stretch of time, and period of history. And that when death and dissolution come to these physical bodies of ours, they come to Us too. All of which these experts relegate to the level of pure poppycock.

How we humans ever got to doing all the poppycock supposing we do about ourselves, our fellow beings, and the rest of the universe is another one of those things that a large percentage of the race has been trying to explain, and with not too conspicuous success, for a long time. Eventually, the averages in such efforts would indicate, each of us, and usually in the hard way, gets around to discovering that if these personal and universal problems are to be solved at all, he will have to go into one of the back rooms of his own mind, or consciousness, so to speak, and solve them himself. As he sincerely goes about doing this, he at once becomes a member in good standing of that unorganizable fellowship of mental and spiritual explorers that has come down from the dim past without interruption, and will continue without interruption, throughout time, space, and even eternity itself.

Speaking personally, most of my poppycock supposing, when I was at peak performance, came from an overload of crystallized, traditional misconceptions about life in general and my own life in particular. And what I supposed into myself and supposed myself into, as a result of these misconceptions, is still something to raise even waxed-down eyebrows. No particular educational system was responsible for this. It came rather from the not uncommon habit of floating about with others of my kind, thinking as they did, doing as they did, and even getting to look as they did, too. Like a machine-cut doughnut, dunking along with other machine-cut doughnuts, through mechanical runways of hot fat.

But I didn't feel too bad about it then, and I don't now, because almost everyone I knew at the time was a human doughnut too. We were all doughnuts.　Differently flavored to be sure, but all doughnuts.　Each of us the product of an exclusive racial, national, social, political, economic, or religious mold.　And each of us dunking compliantly and uniformly along, in true doughnutty fashion, through what would be equivalent to runways of hot fat under the watchful eye of whoever controlled the current and happened to be holding the testing and prodding fork.

*Chapter Twenty-three*

## ABSENTEES

Some centuries ago when, as it would appear from the historical records, human beings were rasslin' with virtually the same individual and collective problems we are rasslin' with today, and getting virtually the same results, one of the greatest of all great mental and spiritual explorers, who, whenever he let drive with anything at anything, really let drive, flung into general human consciousness a metaphysical bomb that has been having repercussions ever since, and especially in these days when so many public and private affairs are so far out of joint. Now a bomb, even in metaphysical form, has to have exceptionally high combustibility in its contents to make an impression that can last for centuries, and this one had that to the 'nth degree.

The timing of it was perfect. And it was aimed, if one reads the old records aright, not so much at those who were sincerely at work on the cosmic obligation to FIND THYSELF . . . KNOW THYSELF . . . BE THYSELF . . . and SHARE THY-

SELF, as it was at the hordes of doughnutty people who, being either too lazy or too indifferent to think for themselves, were dunking and doing in thought, word, and deed, exactly as everyone they associated with was dunking and doing in thought, word, and deed. And doing it perhaps, not so much from personal choice, as from the subtle, direction-pressure manipulation of skilled promoters, representing economic, religious, political, social, and other types of organized numbers-gathering interests.

The fellow who did the flinging was that two-fisted, plain-speaking, utterly fearless, up-and-at-'em Paul of Tarsus. And Paul, you will recall, after making a long series of lurid mistakes in the first part of his career, was good enough at what he subsequently did to win sainthood, as well as the affectionate gratitude of untold millions of men, women, and children. Through his undeviating resolution in following The Light that came to him with such dramatic suddenness on his famous journey to Damascus, plus his rich experience, and plus, too, his refusal to remain in the mistakes he made, either mentally or otherwise, he has become generally recognized as an all-time authority on just what it takes to attain and move in the ongoing harmony and rhythm of celestial living here and now.

[169]

Paul was not only an expert in flinging metaphysical bombs, but also in planting them for contact and time explosion. Even today, centuries
later, his bombs are still going off with sudden and
terrific force in individual minds and hearts, blast-
ing their possessors onto better levels of thinking
and living. The particular bomb I have refer-
ence to in this chapter was neatly wrapped and
tucked inside what on the surface appeared to be
one of those guileless, innocuous paradoxes so
brilliantly produced by those wise Bible characters
whenever they wanted to call the attention of their
fellow beings to some important facet of Truth
that was being generally overlooked.

The contents of the bomb were mostly vocal,
and they were tucked inside the admonition that
one must get out of the human body and stay away
from the human body if he wanted to regain his
divine birthright and experience the ecstasy and
bliss of heavenly living at the present time, instead
of having to wait to die into it. "Being absent
from the body," is the way Paul put it, pointing
out that when one is "at home in the body," he is
"absent from THE LORD," and that when he is "absent from the body," he is "present with THE
LORD."

A modern might paraphrase it this way: when
a spiritually mental BEING of infinite proportions

like YOU tries to identify YOURSELF as a little, restricted, material entity existing inside a human
body, you have permitted an illusion to get in between you and Reality, between you and YOU. By
this practice, you have imprisoned yourself—not
YOURSELF, remember—within an unreal concept
of your own making. By thus being "at home in
the body," you have become "absent from THE
LORD." That is, through this erroneous sense of
things, you have become absent from your individual place and part in the divine ALL-PRESENCE.
An ALL-PRESENCE functioning by its own Intelligence and Power, and through its own Harmony
and Rhythm, all about YOU, in YOU, through YOU,
and as YOU. An ALL-PRESENCE that we moderns
reverently call God, and Paul just as reverently
spoke of as THE LORD.

To all real mental explorers, Paul's admonition
has always been not only a challenge, but an opportunity for moving out in new directions into
larger areas of THEMSELVES. But to those with
little appetite for thinking around outside the
familiar biological ruts and routines, Paul's advice, if they pay any attention to it at all, is a mani-
fest absurdity. For how could anyone possibly be
absent from his body, they reason, and still remain
alive? To them, such absenteeism means only
one thing—death and oblivion. It means the

[171]

final period of everything. But to that high-altitude cruiser—Paul of Tarsus—it meant just the opposite. It meant more expansive living, more abundant living, more satisfying living. It meant swinging full-out into eternal Life, in the present-tenseness of things.

Paul could understand with wisely discriminating sympathy the plight of those fellow beings of his who had incarcerated their sense of themselves in human prison-body concepts, because he had trapped himself in one of them. But having discovered the false nature of this concept, he was able, of course, to take himself out of it, and having done so, to share the open secret of the way out with all who cared to listen to him. It is apparent that it wasn't easy for most of the people of his time to understand him, and this, it would appear, was almost entirely because of a lack of lift in their thoughts and an almost complete absence of imagination. And besides, he was probably far too simple and direct for their complicated and clogged mental entrances.

What caused the crisscross between Paul and so many of those who listened to him, as well as to so many who read him today, is as clear as daylight. He and they were going at life in entirely different directions. He and they were placing value on

[172]

entirely different things.   Paul was advising them
to get mentally out of their bodies, and to stay
mentally outside of their bodies, really to live.
They were coddling, worshipping, and clinging
desperately to their bodies, for fear they wouldn't
live.   Paul was laying the full emphasis of his life
on the mental, the spiritual, the subjective, the
undimensional, and the eternal.   They were placing their emphasis on the physical, the material,
the human, the objective, the limited, the dying,
and the disappearing.

What Paul, with his clarified vision and his
ability to prove the things he knew, was trying
to help all of us grasp and understand, it is now
quite clear, is just what so many other great spiritual thinkers have been trying to help us grasp
and understand: namely, that individual MAN
never has been, is not now, and never can be a
restricted little mortal entity inside a skin-casing,
and subject to extinction at any hour of the day or
night.   But—and with this "but" there is a complete swing-around—that he was, and is, and always will be a spiritually mental being, completely
free from every phase of corporeality and from
every phase of bondage to it.   A spiritually mental being of such vast proportions, they iterated
and reiterated, that he is able to contain within

HIMSELF as part of HIMSELF everything of which he can become aware, up to and including all of the universe he can identify.

That was strong stuff for human beings geared to group-thinking within fixed biological boundaries and according to fixed patterns. They were so enmeshed in the illusion of their material concepts that they had come to regard their human bodies as themselves. Consequently, they were completely sold on the notion that their spans of life and usefulness lasted just as long as they could keep their physical bodies alive and active. The idea that these bodies were nothing more than shadowgraphs that they were projecting and watching in their own minds or consciousness was far too transcendental for their standardized thinking. They believed that to be in existence at all it was necessary to be in something—in a human body, in a building, in a city, in a country, and so on. That they actually contained all these things within THEMSELVES was too inconceivably fantastic. But then, they had their eyes on themselves, not THEMSELVES.

What Paul was obviously trying to do, in that now famous but so little-understood "absent-from-the-body" and "present-with-THE-LORD" admonition of his, was to extricate men and women from being such needless biological shut-ins. To persuade them to quit estimating themselves, their fellows, and the rest of the universe, by the out-wardly visible alone. To impress upon them the great need for mentally exploring through all ma-terial-physical-human forms, symbols, and names, and finding the eternal facts back of them. And having lured or blasted them loose from their petty and futile little biological life patterns that were getting them nowhere at all, to show them with the deft skill of an accomplished performer, and in a spirit of individual high adventure, how to zoom out in the full spread of their spiritually mental beings, and instead of merely existing, do some real living for a change.

*Chapter Twenty-four*

## DUMMIES!

Proficiency in high- and low-altitude acrobatics is just as essential for mental explorers as it is for flying pilots, and probably more so. In aerial acrobatics both mental explorers and flying pilots have opportunities for whipping into perfection the things they have learned in their basic training and experience. Such things, for instance, as alertness, firmness of purpose, courage, flexibility, poise, perception, co-ordination, self-reliance, swift adjustment to the immediate situation, and that intuitive feel of knowing just what to do, no matter what happens. And perhaps more than anything else, the opportunity for proving again and again that the unseen good laws of a perfectly functioning Creator are ever available and ever ready to work with them and for them, whenever they correctly do their part.

As a matter of fact, the techniques of the mental explorer and the flying pilot are so closely interrelated that a good mental explorer, if he has a mind for it, always makes an excellent flying pilot, and a good flying pilot always makes a first-rate mental explorer. Much of this, no doubt, is due to the fact that both of them carry on their more important activities high above the earth-levels, and high above all that those earth-levels symbolize. They both move in stratas of exalted experience, stratas the magnitude and the mental and even physical possibilities of which have thus far only dimly begun to dawn in general human consciousness.

The flying pilot, with his practical knowledge of atmospheric conditions between earth and stratosphere, finding himself in obscuring clouds, or enveloped by a sudden storm, has a simple and effective remedy. He turns the nose of his plane upward, finds the sunshine again, levels off, cruises along in smooth, clear, sweet air in which not only he but even his engine breathes better. The mental explorer does virtually the same thing. Enveloped, let us say, by such low-altitude conditions as discord, disappointment, conflict, confusion, disaster, despair, and other personal and general experiences of trouble that we so frequently symbolize as mist, clouds, and storms, he tips the nose of his all-thinking upward, finds the sunshine again at higher altitudes, levels off, and cruises along in smooth, sweet air, too.

In his high-altitude experience, the flying pilot

[177]

usually undergoes an expansion of consciousness that he finds highly exhilarating and satisfying, but often difficult to explain to others or even to himself. But he feels it, and with it there invariably comes a great sense of release from earth-handicaps in general and his own private problems in particular; of utter freedom, of intimate kinship with everything everywhere. And beyond and above everything else, a breath-taking awareness of a perfect and companionable Intelligence, moving with resistless energy and purpose back of, through, and with everything, including himself. Whether conscious of it or not, he has joined the Universal. Knowingly or unknowingly, he has touched and become one with THAT PRESENCE for which he innately longs, and to which, if he prays at all, he directs his prayers. The spiritual explorer, moving entirely in the realm of thought, arrives at this awareness too, but in a more direct way.

If you were within easy traveling distance of this old garden in Hollywood, California, in which I am arranging these words on paper, and if you had a fancy for such a venture, I could arrange for us to take our bodies to a flying field over in the next valley, place them in a plane, and then, with a highly accomplished flying friend to do the rest, provide you with some real aerial acrobatics. You might enjoy them, and then again you might not.

But one thing is certain, you would not come out of the plane quite as you went into it. Few ever do who go stunting with this particular buckaroo of the air, because of the unorthodox way in which he intermixes and executes spirals, spins, slips, loops, rolls, chandelles, lazy-eights, Immelman turns, power dives, upside-down things, and unnamable inventions of his own.

What prevents the all of you from joining me in this lively enterprise—for of course you can easily do so mentally—are all the man-made, definitely stupid, illusion-beliefs of time, space, physical bodies, and materiality in general, which are supposed to keep us separated from one another, and limited to some specific place and condition in existence. But I'll tell you what I can do in the circumstances. I can set up a kind of mental runway for you, give you a good start toward making altitude with your thoughts, and then let you do some acrobatics on your own. Acrobatics that, if you can get high enough, should provide you with more exciting and satisfying adventures than anything my stunting pilot friend could possibly do for you in his plane.

Let's have a try at the thing! But remember, you are being catapulted into acrobatics, and acrobatics, whether mental or otherwise, are never conventional proceedings either on or off the earth.

[179]

To begin with, place that body of yours in a comfortable position, if possible in a rocking chair. Then put the oil can to your have-fun joints. Next, take all the wraps off your imagination. Having accomplished that, let your thinking spread to its fullest circumference. When you arrive at what you consider your greatest mental height, breadth, and depth, pause for as much time as you can devote to it, and with reverence and humble teachableness contemplate the almost unbelievable vastness of territory that that thinking of yours is covering and including. Then remind yourself again and again, as has so often been suggested in these pages, that all that enormous expanse and everything within that enormous expanse is not only part of You, but actually is You!

At that level of mental attainment, you would have what the flying pilot, in his world of activity, would call good altitude for stunting. With this in mind, let's call that vast and unboundable sweep of the real mental You—Edgar Bergen. And that human body of yours—Charlie McCarthy. That is, the mental You is the ventriloquist, and your human body is the dummy. The acrobatics now begin! So sit loose, my Hearty, and be sure to wrap your legs around something, for almost anything can happen to you within the next few minutes! But in these acrobatics you should at least

[180]

get a clearer understanding of why it is that that human body you have is yours but not You. And why it is, too, that you have such absolute dominion over the thing, if you but knew it, and then made use of that knowledge.

Now Charlie McCarthy, though internationally famous and a very popular and amusing young fellow, as you so well know, and though seeming to be very much alive and capable of carrying on all sorts of rational and sophisticated activities, is a dummy all the way through. But so is that human body of yours. Speaking quite impersonally, the difference between them is merely one of materials. A ventriloquist's inanimate dummy is mostly wood, and costs—when carved, painted, and dressed—anywhere between $25 and $500. That dummy of yours that you use in your everyday experience is made up of highly perishable and breakable material substances, chemicals, and a few other things, and in an inanimate state, and without clothes, is worth between seventy-five and eighty-seven cents.

What Charlie McCarthy is in appearance, in intelligence, in manners, in behavior, and in accomplishment, he is by the grace of Edgar Bergen, who uses him merely as a tool, or rather as an instrument by which and through which to express himself. What that human body, or dummy, of yours is in appearance, in intelligence, in manners, in behavior, and in accomplishment, it is by the grace of the mental You. It is nothing more than the tool, or instrument, you use to express yourself in this shadowgraph show that you and all the rest of us are helping to put on, to sustain, and then to watch. Where Edgar Bergen has an edge with Charlie McCarthy is that whenever he gets bored with that particular dummy, he can throw it into a trunk, forget it, and go on having just as good a time with life.

No matter how realistic or important Charlie McCarthy and that physical body of yours may seem to become, they will always be dummies, re-gardless of how much slicking up and attention they get. Charlie McCarthy moves about, thinks, talks, sings, wisecracks, behaves, and misbehaves only because Edgar Bergen is doing the animating, the thinking, and the vocalizing. The mental You does precisely the same thing with that dummy-body of yours. Without Edgar Bergen's nimble mind, his slit-mouth voice, and his fingers on the controls, Charlie McCarthy would be what my good friend Sid Grauman—one of the world's greatest theatrical impresarios—would call "a com-plete floparoo!" Without the mental You, ani-mating and speaking through that flesh-dummy of yours, it would be what Mr. Grauman, reaching for an extreme one in his colorful and unorthodox language, would call "a busto-crusto!" And beyond that, let it be noted, there is no degree of nothingness.

"Nonsense, twaddle, and madness!" says you, perhaps! Well, that depends entirely on your outlook. If you are accustomed to worming along earthly levels and estimating life from an angleworm's angle, the answer of course is "Yes!" But if you are mentally up and out where you belong— that is, up and out in the fullness of your real individual being—the answer is exactly the opposite. And the more mental and spiritual acrobatics you do, high above those dark, dull, and dreary material senses of yours, the more you will come to realize the importance of always making a clean-cut distinction between the illusion of that material and human you and the eternal reality of that spiritually mental You. And the more you realize this, the more you will relegate that physical body of yours to its proper place—that of a concept, a dummy, a tool, and treat it as such.

Then comes the most reassuring and comforting fact of all. This: that even though you should seem to be deprived of that human body of yours, that dummy, and even though all the medical men, coroners, and undertakers in the world should pronounce you dead and extinct, You would still be a

spiritually mental BEING!   Still be alive and flourishing!   Still be YOURSELF!   Still be a distinct
IDENTITY in an ever-living, ever-harmoniously
functioning universe!   Still be a SOMEBODY!   Still
be an important FACT and FACTOR in a fascinating
creation.   Still be You!   And You would know
it, regardless of what seemed to be happening to
the human you, to others, or to the world at large,
in the human shadowgraph show.

## Chapter Twenty-five

## INTERLUDES

Well, my Hearty, as acrobatic adventurers having looks at life from uncommon angles of observation, you and I may have ousted these material bodies of ours from their imposing dictatorial thrones, at least theoretically. And we may have unceremoniously reduced them to the status of dummies, worth—unclothed and unanimated—you will remember, between seventy-five and eighty-seven cents undelivered. And we may have established them in our individual minds as mere tools or instruments by which and through which we express ourselves in this shadowgraph show that the orthodox-minded call human existence. But that isn't all there is to it by a long shot! We are still nose-flattened, mentally speaking, against another phase of the same problem, and that is the problem of self; but self spelled with a small "s," and having to do with the physical-material-human sense of existence.

Trying to understand self is by no means easy, either as an undertaking or an accomplishment.

One usually begins the effort more or less casually and in uniform step with the kind of people he moves about with, provided it isn't too arduous or doesn't interfere too much with his private pleasures. But before he is through with some of the somersaulting he inevitably will undergo in his human experience, he is apt to be struggling with that self from bent knees and with a bowed head. Trying to estimate correctly, and particularly trying to know just what to do and what not to do with self in public and private living, has ever been one of humanity's most puzzling and baffling quandaries. And definitely its most "continuing pain in the neck," which, almost any free-talking gent will assure you, can symbolize anything from wispy annoyance to the most afflictive and grievous of torments to mind, body, or estate.

Speaking broadly and generally, the most popular way, down through the centuries, for dealing with this tantalizing perplexity, has been to invent means by which, in which, or through which the individual could get away from himself and forget himself for a while. Hence the e-nor-mous!—as a circus barker would put it—output of almost every conceivable type of so-called escape literature, plays, movies, and other forms of eye and ear entertainment. Hence too, the widespread use of alcohol, drugs, and other concoctions for stimu-

[186]

lating or soothing the would-be escapist and thus helping him forget for a while.

Hence also the reason for the uncountable thousands upon thousands of amateur and professional "how to" writers, lecturers, consultants, and advisers holding forth, usually at so much per, all over the world. An amazing, unorganized army, containing within its ranks almost every imaginable type of human being, ranging all the way from Christlike men and women, capable of living and proving the things they talk about, to clever, slick-talking, inwardly insincere pretenders, opportunists, promoters, racketeers, petty crooks, and shysters who prey for profit.

But forgetting them for the moment, how common to all of us is the experience of getting fed up with one another and with everyday experience, and then in a state of seething annoyance, discontent, and discouragement, seeking to forget it all with an interlude. Now an interlude, Mr. Webster and his associates will inform you, if you care to thumb through their dictionary, was originally "an entertainment of a light or farcical character, introduced between the acts of the old mystery and morality plays. . . ." Private versions of which, I am sure you will agree with me, each of us is putting on continuously in his own life. It also means, according to Mr. W. and his associates,

[187]

"any form of intervening or interruptive space, feature, or event."

These interludes of escape that humans have invented for themselves include almost everything imaginable, from the most transcendent aspirations to bizarre ways of ending one's existence. That the race has survived most of them is clear proof that the spark of divinity actually does exist in us. A compilation of these ways out might start, for instance, with merely wasting precious time that might have been spent in improvement and accomplishment in unnecessary sleep or daydreaming. Or by floating around in a time-killing, unwise indiscretion. Or by reading cheap and degrading fiction about defectives. Or by watching equally cheap and degrading movies, plays, and other forms of drugging and life-distorting entertainment. Or by getting drunk with alcohol or sex. Or by flinging one's self into some highly regimented, emotionally supercharged crowd activity and permitting others to think for one. And so on, *ad infinitum!*

Seeking some form of interlude by means of which to forget, and in that forgetting find temporary release from the pressure of trying to keep alive, well, happy, prosperous, and morally stabilized, has ever been both a common urge and a common problem. But how common is the ex-

[188]

perience, too, of returning from one of these personally conducted interludes, either light, medium, or heavy, to find the same old self that we had gone to such efforts to get rid of waiting for us right where we left it and as we left it, and silently and insolently demanding, "Well, what do we do now?"

Trying to escape from self by the interlude method, only to have the same old self we left behind come bouncing back into experience again after the interlude, with the same problems we thought we had buried, drowned, or otherwise destroyed, is just about as annoying a kickback from applied effort as one can receive. For we find ourselves right back where we started from, only more involved. The experts in spacious and gracious living, exceedingly wise in matters of this kind, insist that kickbacks from interludes of this nature are exceedingly good for us. They call them warning signals of danger ahead, cautioning us that while our purpose in wanting to escape may be a commendable one, our methods of doing so need brisk and immediate improving.

As far back as man's origin goes, say these experts, as far back as that has man been hoping, wishing, longing, struggling, fighting, praying, and searching for ways to escape from his restlessness and discontent with existence as he finds it. And

[189]

particularly has he striven for ways to get away from the seen and unseen things that shut him off from being what he feels he has a right to be, from doing what he feels he has a right to do, and from having what he feels he has a right to have. The number and combinations of numbers of things he has tried, in an effort to achieve escape, and to find enduring happiness, peace, and satisfaction, have been more than anyone could possibly count. "And yet," ask the experts tossing the matter into each of our individual laps, "is man any nearer to solving the problem of escape today? Are you any nearer to solving it for yourself today?"

If you had no answers ready, and you would have to have not only good, but demonstrable answers for these experts, you would, if your feelings in the matter were beyond the lukewarm stage, deposit that body of yours in a quiet place and do some private and personal thinking, or meditating, or introspection, or communing, or praying, or whatever you like to call such mental intake and outgo efforts. As you did this with sufficient humility, teachableness, and receptivity, you couldn't help becoming aware that what you regarded as yourself was extending not only immeasurably beyond your human boundaries, but immeasurably beyond all material conditions as well. And moreover, that this physically unseeable, expanding self was a contributing part in a vast, physically unseeable, but mentally recognizable, harmoniously functioning universe that had never been interrupted in the slightest degree because of its eternal nature.

With that inner knowledge you could soar high and wide, but the probabilities are that, as you did so, some thought having to do with the things you left behind you would shoot across your mental view, send you into a tailspin, and bring you back again to earth with its tottering civilization, the widespread chaos and misery throughout the world, and your own assortment of problems. But even flattened out on the earth and smudged with earthly conditions, you would still be a mental explorer, and as such you would want to know the reason for the tottering, the chaos, the misery, and your own private difficulties.

As you diligently searched with teachable receptivity, I believe you would unearth a tremendously important clew. And the base of it would be embedded in the simple but usually difficult-to-see fact that a most essential something was flickering low, if not actually going out, in individual and group thinking, and consequently in individual and group living. A something we used to call individual character, once upon a time. A something that, when broken up into its component

[191]

parts, includes such inherent excellences as purity
. . . sincerity . . . joy . . . friendliness . . . fun-
. . . unselfishness . . . laughter . . . love . . .
faith . . . goodness . . . or totaled together—
Godlikeness.

Knowing, as you would know, of course, that all
Creation functions through and by means of the
individual unit, you would know what had to be
done about the situation, as far as you were concerned. For you would recognize, as have all the
great mental and spiritual adventurers, that every
personal, group, national, world, and universal
problem has of necessity to be reduced to the individual self—that is, to the individual mind, or
consciousness—and therein either solved or left
unsolved. Which is why, you would note with
ever-increasing satisfaction, you were always in a
position to solve any difficulty anywhere, without
having to go there to do it, except mentally and
spiritually.

At which point any need you might have felt
you had for interludes would have completely disappeared. For you would have been seeing, with
something far more penetrating and observing
than human eyes, that the only way to escape from
the ills, the tediousness, the troubles, and the
wants and woes of self is not by ducking away from
self, or by struggling with self, or by punishing

self, or by being sorry for self, but by swinging one's entire self outward and upward, and attaining SELF. Or in other words, enlarging, improving, and enriching the mental self until it expands into the spiritual SELF. And the attainment of that would be compliance with the ancient admonition to FIND THYSELF . . . KNOW THYSELF . . . BE THYSELF . . . and SHARE THYSELF.

*Chapter Twenty-six*

## EXPANSION

Let us veer off a bit in these unconventional adventures of ours in quest of what John Bunyan in his immortal *Pilgrim's Progress* metaphorically called "the Delectable Mountains," from whose summit, you will recall, "the Celestial City" was visible, as well as the best and most direct route for getting there. Or to make it more modern-dayish, in this unorthodox attempt of ours to get to that elevation of awareness from which we can begin to understand the whence, the why, and the whither of ourselves, our community, our country, our world, and our universe, and what to do about them all to bring about more harmony, we should, according to the best charts and graphs, do some back-tracking, you doing yours in your life, I doing mine in my life.

If you like the idea, may I suggest that you follow the customary procedure: park your body in some pleasing place and position, empty yourself of all problems the way a truck upends and dumps its load, and then take off mentally, making all the altitude you can, in order to see as much of your personal terrain as possible. But this time, instead of moving in the direction of your most distant horizon point, head back through your past life. Go as far back into your public and private history as your memory will take you; and as one explorer ever interested in knowing what's behind and beyond everything that exists to another explorer ditto ditto, I hope your memory is stretchable enough to take you, clear-visioned, not only back to your human birth, but through it and into your pre-existence.

As you set your compass directions and head back, scrutinize closely for clews and evidence of whatever appears within your range of vision, regardless of how insignificant it may seem. Then, as you mentally hedgehop along, investigating yourself at first hand, make a list of everything you find that made you a bigger, better, and more useful person, at least temporarily, as you came in contact with it, or perhaps as it came in contact with you. The list should include not only the people you have known, the places you have visited, and the things you have read, listened to, and looked at, but everything else that in any way infused into you more of what is enduringly beautiful, good, and true.

The first time I tried this kind of back-tracking

research, I wrecked a large and much cherished framework on which for many years I had been displaying, even professionally, my notions of real values. It so happens that as a writer, a motion picture executive and producer, and, for want of a better term, an international look-arounder, I was privileged to live, and in a most intimate way, in some of the world's most colorful and exciting centers when, it is generally agreed among those in the know, they were at peak expression in color and excitement. Such centers, for instance, as Newport, Rhode Island, New York, Boston, Philadelphia, Washington, San Francisco, Hollywood, London, Paris, Berlin, Rome, Algiers, Cairo, Shanghai, Tokio, Bali, and others too numerous to tack on here.

Please be assured that this travelogue effect is not recounted in any attempt to burn incense to myself, I'll cross my heart on that, but merely to establish the point that when I started the adventure back into myself I was heading back through a memory crowded with unusual places visited, unusual people known, and unusual experiences lived through. The idea of it began innocently and simply enough. I merely started trying to recall by way of self-entertainment, as I lay in the sun on an isolated beach, just who and what in my past had enriched and influenced my life for the better.

I went back at slow speed over hundreds upon hundreds of interviews I had had as a newspaperman, with men and women in different countries, who, for the time being at least, were either famous or infamous. The scope of the journey by memory was wide, for my editors sent me after almost everyone everywhere who had enough push, wiggle, and glitter to get above the flat levels of average rutty and routine existence and show promise of being what they considered interesting copy. Exhausting this array of famous and infamous ones, I next combed through all the men and women with nationally and internationally known names whom I had known socially here and abroad, or had been associated with in the theatre, in motion pictures, and other mediums of public expression.

Then came the bolt from the blue! A bolt that whammed straight down through the middle of my setup of values, wrecked the whole thing, and brought what I then regarded as "me" to earth with a crash that is still vividly memorable. For strange as it may appear, with certain conspicuous exceptions, I could not recall to mind— and I have a fairly good recaller—one thing that any of these famous men and women had told me for publication or in private that had in any way really lifted, broadened, or deepened my thinking, or given me any new compass directions with which to navigate my own life better. Nor could I remember one thing that any of them had done away from their particular specialty in public performance that had left any lasting inspiration either. True, they had been impressive in a transitory way, in the way and the mood of the moment, and often terrifically so. But what virtually all of them had been diffusing, I suddenly realized, lacked what a great mind once called "the pollen of immortality."

It was a dramatically deflating anticlimax for my assortment of celebrities, but it was for me too, as I had to begin all over again and find new values. When I had sufficiently recovered from the upset, I began another search back through experience, but this time without the handicap of the celebrities, the big shots, and the other types of publicity and applause hunters. This time I began where I should have started in the first place: I began with the most genuine and influential-for-the-better person I have ever known—my little Rhode Island mother. Using the simple interrogation: "What happened here by way of improving my thinking and living?" I moved out mentally from my mother, and revisited just people, and animals, and birds, and books, and plays, and insects, and paintings, and musical occasions, and hours with nature and such things. It was an amazing revelation of values. Of real and enduring values. Of values that had been generously shared with me, but that I had allowed to become covered with the dust of neglect, and for which I had forgotten to be grateful.

As I took time to study these values, I made what for me was a most beneficial discovery. The first part of it was this: In every instance, I could see, as I looked back at them correctly, those values had been the spontaneous outflowing of divinely flavored inner elegance and goodness, expressions, I remembered, that had poured from whomever or whatever the humanly visible source happened to be, like song from a bird, perfume from a flower, and laughter from a child; and thus of necessity blessing everything that came within the radius of its influence. And the second part of the discovery came from the fact that every time I had been exposed to one of these values, my thinking and being had been expanded, and in that expansion I had always moved out more into the flow and glow of real living, and generally without being aware that the miracle had taken place.

When I got my mental fingers on that word "expansion," and some of the synonyms that keep company with it, I had the answer to many why's that had long been puzzling me. For instance,

[199]

why it is that so many nobodies, ordinary things, common incidents, and very familiar fellows outside the human species had been able to leave such useful and enduring values with me, and so many famous men and women hadn't been able to do so at all.    Why it is too, that down through the centuries the flavor and memory of certain individuals, books, plays, music, paintings, poetry, and so on have been of such continuous benefit to mankind, while so many others are such impermanent flashes in the pan.    And with that word "expansion" as the basis of the recipe, it was plain to see that all individual human effort in the future will either have to have this divinely flavored ingredient of expansion in it, and in that expansion, ways and means of helping others live more abundantly, or be a failure like all the rest.

The reason for this is apparent.    Within each one of us is a never-satisfied hunger for greater freedom of being and expression, and with it an almost constant urge to find new ways to get more out of life, ways that will be more productive and satisfying than those offered by the material senses. This, all the great spiritual teachers agree, is the manifestation and the stir of the divine within us, and the proof that we cannot escape the perfection predestined for each one of us; because, as they point out, we each happen to be part of it,

[200]

regardless of whether we have awakened to the fact or not. Hence, they add significantly, our instinctive and enthusiastic response to whomever or whatever expands us outward, upward, and onward toward these true spiritual proportions.

# Chapter Twenty-seven

## AXIOM

There is an ancient axiom that each of us human earth-riders encounters sooner or later, as he moves out, according to his sense of things, to be more of what he would like to be, or at least ought to be. An axiom that those who work with humanity to make something better come out of it, if possible, have used in almost every known thematic form, from gentle essays and sermons to moral shillalahs with which to clout obdurate persons on their nonresponsive pates. An axiom that always provides an excellent taking-off point for private expeditions into the jungles of one's own mind—jungles, as you probably know, now being regarded more as individual states of mind than geographical locations. And the axiom is this: that no one ever finds human life much worth living, or the human world in which he finds himself much worth living in; he has to make them so.

It's a simple-sounding but terribly embarrassing little axiom, for it forces each of us, whether we like the idea or not, to accept responsibilities it is always so much more satisfying to unload on someone else, or an assortment of other people, provided, of course, that we can get away with it with good grace. But those who have been the most trustworthy guides and counsellors to mankind down through the ages say that such evasion is utterly impossible, and that mankind's attempt to unload his responsibilities in the past as well as at the present time is responsible for virtually all the difficulties and woes in which we find ourselves today. That the material human world is in a deplorable massed-up mess is generally agreed to by all the modern experts in these matters. And when it comes to placing the blame for this shocking and continuing state of affairs, they are in general agreement, too.

Down through history, as you have undoubtedly observed in your mental adventurings around, the popular method for accounting for most of our public and private trouble has been to hunt for causes as far removed, and as much unrelated to ourselves and our particular grouping of selves, as possible. And of these, the most favored repository of blame has been unseen evil forces, anciently personified by the devil, that operated from a base—supposedly "up there somewhere," or "out yonder somewhere," or most supposedly of all, "down below somewhere." These sinister forces, according to the traditionally popular belief, operate through stars, prearranged fate, conditions, circumstances, people, groups, nations, in fact through almost everything except one's own self, and ceaselessly conspire against man's individual goodness, peace of mind, happiness, and success.

But these wide-ranging mental explorers, cruising high above such superstition and mesmerism, go at the matter from an entirely different angle. "There is only one thing wrong with you, and your everyday existence, and the world," they say in substance, aiming their remarks at each of us and not pulling their moral punches in the least. "And it isn't any unavoidable, predestined fate moving against you in particular as its victim. And it isn't unfriendly people whom you may believe have it in for you and your kind. And it isn't antagonistically inclined organized groups, institutions, communities, races, religions, and other regimented combinations with which you are not affiliated. The only thing wrong with the situation in whole, or in part, is you! Just you! No one else. Nothing else. Just you!"

They don't quibble about this in the least. "Stop blaming other people and other things for your own and the world's woes!" they are flinging

[204]

at you and me and the other fellow from out of the depths of their seasoned wisdom and experience. "It's not what some other person, or even a nationful of them, is thinking, or believing, or saying, or doing! It's what you, and you alone, are thinking, and believing, and saying, and doing that counts! For remember, you are an individual! You are a distinct, complete, living, and thinking identity! You are You! And not only are you You, but You are your own world and your own universe. You include them within that truly marvelous mind of yours, where, don't ever forget, you have charge of all the thinking that goes on. And until you discover this fact, and fully accept its responsibilities, you are likely to continue to find your life not much worth the living, and your particular world and universe quite undesirable places."

Their conviction about this seems to come from two closely related facts that apparently enter into everything they do. The first one is this: that Life, regardless of all ground observations to the contrary, is a spiritually mental, universal, illimitable, indivisible, uninterruptible process. A process in which diversity and unity are one. And the second: that creation, in every phase of its vast totality, functions through the individual life, thus making each life an important and necessary factor in the Creator's plan and purpose. But it is a plan and purpose, they are always swift to point out, in which each individual either accepts his obligations, lives constantly at his best, and moves in harmonious and rhythmical togetherness with everything everywhere, or goes through some form of needed discipline until he does.

What they are so well aware of, it is clearly evident from the things they say, write, and otherwise do, is what all the outstanding thinkers throughout history have been keenly aware of, too; and that is this: that the perfecting of the individual life is the fundamental basis of all well-being, all progress, and all happiness. Hence, that the group, the nation, and even the world itself can flourish only when and as the individual flourishes. And that when individuality starts to fade, wither, and deteriorate—that is, when it begins to lose its clearcut identity, its independence in being and thinking and doing, and begins merging itself in the mass, then down of necessity goes the group, the nation, and the world too.

Fortunately for the rest of us, however, they do not let the matter remain as a philosophical abstraction. They know that something very definite and immediate has to be done, if individuality is to be saved from disappearing into a total eclipse, and perhaps plunging mankind into more dark ages, and they know what that something is. It is to by-pass the human in his various herd formations, and to appeal to him one by one, as an individual, on a "come-out-from-among-them-and-be-ye-separate" basis. Or in other words, to reach the individual through whatever method he can best understand, and help him discover what he was divinely designed to be, and what the world so desperately needs him to be, especially at the present time.

This new and yet old campaigning—and in its operation it is as subtle as it is wise and fruitful—is apparent everywhere today, if one's perceptive faculties are sharp enough to detect it. You can hear it emanating from private and public speech. You will find it percolating through books, magazines, newspapers, plays, the radio, and even, believe it or not, politics. It is the spontaneous, individual effort of mentally and spiritually free men and women, of men and women of exceedingly good will, to help others become mentally and spiritually free too. And they are doing this, not by forcing their individual beliefs and theories on the other fellow, or by persuading him to join something and subscribe to certain doctrines, but by trying to make the other fellow aware of the universally important things going on within his mind and heart, and then encouraging him to turn all of himself on, and pour himself out in universal expression for the universal good, usually reminding him that each of us is worth only what he inwardly possesses.  Only what he inwardly has to share.

## Chapter Twenty-eight

## SWEEPING ON

A few more pages, my Hearty, and then, for better or worse, you come and yet don't come to the end of this book. On the surface that sounds both ambiguous and silly, but as has already been pointed out, while this book has what is technically known as a beginning, it has no ending in the usual meaning of that term. When you reach what is supposed to be the back cover, you go sweeping right through that phenomenon with, I trust, just as much rhythm and ease as characterized the man on the flying trapeze. Then, having done that, you are supposed to keep sweeping on under your own horsepower and pilotage throughout time, space, and even eternity itself. That is, you do so, as was also pointed out, provided you have accumulated sufficient mental velocity, altitude, and visibility to permit it.

Among the more discerning and discriminating ones riding the earth today who are ably qualified to know what they are talking about, it is generally agreed that for any book to justify itself in these

tumultuous and difficult times of worldwide social, political, and economic readjustments, when
the old selfish ways of thinking and living are
cracking up like river ice before the spring floods,
when personal integrity and goodwill are at such
low ebb, and when we humans are having to learn
in the hard way to be more universal in our interests, sympathies, and loyalties—it is generally
agreed, as I started to say, that you, the reader,
are entitled to the utmost respect and consideration. And not the least of these considerations,
they maintain, should be the opportunity for you
to gather enough fresh and generating momentum
as you read so that when you go through a back
cover you can sweep out clear-visioned and more
understandingly into larger and more delightful
areas in your thinking and living.

Thus too, they insist, should you be able to
sweep through and beyond all stage plays, movies,
radio performances, and other entertainment;
through and beyond all forms and symbols in art
and music; through and beyond, in fact, every
known type of individual and group expression.
For the only justification for any expression aimed
in the direction of your eyes and ears, they declare,
is its effort to help and bless you; to make you a
happier and more useful citizen of your community, of your nation, of your world, of your uni-

verse, and of eternity. And if this motive-ingredi-
ent be lacking, they warn, then look out! for
something insidious and dangerous is at work trying to plug up your mental and spiritual inlets
and outlets, and to undermine your foundations.

As you mentally tail-by the last page in this
book, headed out for only you know where, it is
a natural hope that at least something in these
pages has brought a measure of entertainment, of
reassurance, and of inspiration. But more than
anything else, I hope, yes, and even pray too, that
you have been able to come upon some new clew
or some new proof that has given you a clearer
realization of your worth and importance as an
individual, and especially of the world's desperate
need for you to do more thinking and living in
that capacity.

Knowing how badly original mental adventurers and explorers are needed today, I will be most
gratified if anything said in these pages has given
you greater determination to move out strictly on
your own, and strictly in your own way, to find
. . . and to know . . . and to be . . . and to share
more of that real SELF of yours. But even if the
book should leave you with a sense of being a cold,
boiled potato, even should you regard it as another one of those things, and yourself as having
dropped far zeroward as a result of exposure to it,

there is one thing worth pasting in your hat and looking at frequently. This: that as you move on in your lone and unavoidable expedition, in which you are the adventurer and the adventure You, there is an overwhelming muchness in your favor.

To begin with, you are alive. And that's a big point in your favor. For another, there is no one else like you anywhere. There never has been, there never will be. Your thumbprints will prove that for you, and establish the fact that you have a definite place and a definite work to do in the universal plan and purpose. For still another thing—and this is a tremendous factor in your favor—you can think. There are no rims around your thinking, except those you clamp on yourself. You are equipped and you are privileged to think about what you please, as you please, and when you please, even though you may not dare to speak and act accordingly. And with that aliveness, that individuality, and that thinking ability, you have the key to everything with you all the time. All the great spiritual thinkers will confirm this for you.

As that living, individualized, thinking You moves out in the direction of your full circumference, following the best compass directions you know how to set, and ever exploring, exploring,

[212]

and exploring, you will always be finding a larger and more interesting SELF to explore, charter, and utilize. As you move farther out, the seeming borders of that SELF move farther out too. It's fascinating! You never catch up with your own individual boundary lines. As you approach them they spread into larger magnitudes. Experiencing this, it will not be in the least difficult for you to realize that your individual capacity for expanding . . . receiving . . . knowing . . . containing . . . being . . . experiencing . . . enjoying . . . expressing . . . and sharing is boundless. And knowing that, you will know for all eternity to come that nothing is impossible for you, nothing too good to be true.

Like all mental explorers who take off from their little finite selves, to find and enjoy more of their larger SELVES, who move out into the darkness to try and make it luminous, you will find plenty of adventure waiting for you every thought of the way. It will not be easy much of the time —few great achievements ever are easy—but you will find it richly rewarding, if you can manage to keep yourself going in the right direction. As you hold to your course, you are likely to find yourself in a more or less constant state of astonished wonder and humble appreciation. And of all these wonderments, few will top the fact that no matter to what prodigious distances you expand that thinking of yours, or what you become aware of in that thinking, everything is taking place inside, not outside, your own individual mind, your own individual consciousness.

The quiet, uninterrupted contemplation of that meaningful truth for awhile ought to give almost any of us, no matter how case-hardened, a profound sense of his obligations, responsibilities, and opportunities as an individual thinker. It should also open up all sorts of clear vistas as to what each of us can do, and has to do, if the world is ever to be brought into a state even remotely resembling unity and moral balance. But even if it didn't do that for us, it ought at least to give us some inkling as to why it is that practically all the great spiritual thinkers have laid such constant stress on the need for individual self-discovery, individual self-knowledge, and individual self-reformation. "You are not in the world," certain of them used to say with challenging emphasis, "you are not in the world, nor the world in you, YOU ARE THE WORLD!"

Life, you will find as you mentally move out into It with your receptive faculties wide open, will more and more reveal Itself to you as a highly intelligent . . . vitalizing . . . beautifying . . . sustaining . . . friendly . . . co-operating ALL-

[214]

PRESENCE. What you call this great ALL-EM-BRACING PRESENCE isn't of major importance, say saint and sage alike. But what is important, they declare, is that you recognize and feel this PRESENCE, that you synchronize your full being with It, and flow along with It. And as you do this, they say, you will come to see with something far more important and enduring than human eyes that neither Life as a whole, nor your individual expression of It, can possibly have such things as boundaries, or limits, or final meanings, or endings, because of its spiritually mental and eternal nature.

*Chapter Twenty-nine*

## ON YOUR BEAM

There are many things that the mental explorer in his rocking chair and the aviator in his plane have in common, as they move outward and upward in their " 'twixt-wanton-earth-and-blessed-heaven" ventures, and one of them in particular I should like to call to your attention as you move through this last chapter and prepare to wing-on for whatever experiences await you beyond. And that is the importance that both mental explorer and aviator place on making contact with their individual beams that are to direct them to their respective objectives. And having found the beams, of the still greater importance of staying on them, regardless of what happens above, below, or around them, until they reach their objectives.

If you were to ask a well-seasoned flyer in a formal and academic way just what he meant by "getting on his beam" and "staying on his beam," and you looked like a fairly good audience, he would no doubt give you a formal and academic earful, beginning with the early pioneering days of the Wright brothers, and coming down to the latest bulletin from his particular flying group. And it is reasonable to assume that you would get some highly interesting technical details about the millions of miles of aerial radio beams, or invisible highways, throughout the United States, extending from all points to all other points and providing aviators with directions by which to navigate their planes accurately and safely from wherever they want to start from to wherever they want to go. And to do so regardless of weather conditions and visibility.

If, however, you knew an aviator well enough to ask him to cut out the technical stuff, and tell you in a simple way and in his own words just what an aerial beam actually does for a flyer, he would quite likely tell you something after the manner in which my rootin', tootin', highfalootin' flying instructor—Eddie Anderson—told me the first time I asked him. "The beam," said the colorful Anderson, throwing his words in almost every direction except mine, as he supervised the preparation of a new plane for a test flight, "is something awfully important going on up there!" Stabbing one of his thumbs skyward, by way of illustration. "You don't see it, or feel it, or touch it, or taste it! You can only hear it! It's something you listen to when you're off the earth! It's a voice! A

[217]

voice that tells you when you're on the right aerial highway and headed in the right direction! If you listen to it, like a good little boy, and if you go in the direction it tells you to go, also like a good little boy, you usually arrive at your destination! If you don't listen to it and follow its instructions, you're likely to make unpleasant headlines!"

On the other hand, if you were to pull a rocking chair alongside that of an experienced mental explorer, and could persuade him to open up and share some of his adventures with you, you would hear him use the term "following his beam," or the equivalent to it, again and again as he told you of the discoveries he had made while exploring the uncharted back country of his own mind, or consciousness. And as you gave close heed to the meaning back of the words he used, you would become increasingly aware of the great emphasis he too was placing on that invisible guiding beam of his, that voice that kept him headed successfully and happily in the right mental and spiritual direction when he listened and obeyed it, but precipitated him into all kinds of besetting difficulties when he didn't.

You can never get lost, and so into trouble, come darkness, fog, cloud, rain, or hail, any good air pilot will tell you, provided you are in contact with

your beam and are implicitly following its directions. Neither can you get lost and into per-
manent difficulties in your everyday experience,
any good mental explorer will assure you, provided you have acquired the technique of being
able to listen to your individual beam-voice. And
provided, too, that you are giving it the same degree of disciplined attention and obedience that
the air pilot does to his radio-beam-voice.

Many and varied, indeed, have been the names
and terms conferred upon this beam-voice down
through the centuries. And wide and varied, too,
have been the ways that human beings have tried
to use it for themselves and others. Many of
them thought of and symbolized this unseen force
as light of one kind or another that appeared in
their individual and collective darkness and gave
illumined guidance. But to most of the great
mental explorers this guiding beam—like that of
the aviators—always came as a voice. Like that
potent, eloquent "still, small voice," for instance,
that the prophet Elijah on top of Mount Horeb,
and in what looked like plenty of trouble, was able
to hear above the wind, the earthquake, the fire,
and all the other physical-material-human phenomena that were trying to get him off his beam
and off his course.

Virtually all these outstanding men and women

whose lives have been recorded attributed this inner beam-voice to their God-source, to that creative and governing Intelligence and Energy back of all manifestations of real being and life.  Never to anything originating within themselves.  They regarded it as a personal and intimate collaboration with God, with God on the sending end and them on the receiving end.  And this beam-voice, you will observe, if you study their lives, communicated with them continuously in simple, understandable, soundless language, telling them just what to do about every detail of their lives and how to do it most effectively; success or failure in each instance, you would also observe, depending on their individual receptivity and willingness to follow instructions.

What you call your particular beam-voice is, of course, a matter for you, and you alone, to decide. The wise thing, the experts say, is to call it what best helps you to grasp and to understand how it operates in all its relations with you.  The great spiritual achievers usually spoke of it in such terms as The Voice of God, The Christ, Revelation, Illumination, Insight, and so on.  The American Indian, with his keen sense of the practicality of The Big Holy, calls it in-hearing and in-knowing.  The fellow with a diploma tags it with such terms as intuition, perception, inspiration, impression, awareness, immediate knowledge, discernment, instinct, comprehension, and so on. The man who likes to say "the most-a in the least-a" calls it a hunch, even though he may not know how to define the term, or understand in the least how the hunch gets from its source to where he can recognize it and use it to do some good for himself.

At which point the entire situation again reverts to you, and to your unavoidable cosmic adventure of having to find more of You . . . know more of You . . . be more of You . . . and share more of You. And it reverts to you in that inner self-consultation chamber of yours, where you ask yourself, or at least I hope you do, how, from this point on, you can best make contact with your own beam-voice, and let it guide you into larger and more satisfying areas of You. In the earsplitting clatter and din of the world's brawling and bawling, and especially with the widespread and growing effort by both seen and unseen agencies to get you off your beam, rob you of your individuality and its expression, and force you to think and act as others want you to think and act, it isn't easy. But it can be done, and sooner or later, you will come to find out, it has to be done by each one of us.

If you were suddenly to become acquainted with

[221]

all the advice that has been given on this important subject, you could fairly well sum it up by saying that your guiding beam-voice is always your loftiest ideal, your finest aspiration. And that this beam-voice becomes clear and available only as you move with all of you in the direction of your highest perfection. Only as you are willing to sacrifice everything to attain this perfection. Which simply means doing the best you can where you are, as you are, with whatever you have to do it with. As you honestly and consistently do your best—and the doing will put you on your beam—you will find, as have all mental explorers, that your way becomes increasingly illuminated and easy to travel, and all your efforts increasingly, blessed. For then, you see, you will be moving out and around in an understanding way, as a receiving and contributing partner in a most delectable universe, wherein all things really do work together for good.

And so as you come to the last period in this book, which is there to stop a sentence but not you; and as you mentally continue on your adventurous way into larger and ever more delightful areas of You, be assured of this enduring fact: that nothing whatsoever can really slow you down, limit your achievements in any right direction, deprive you of your well-being and fun in living, or in any way stop your successful ongoing, but you yourself. For remember, you are alive. You can think. You are a self-contained, individual entity. You have something to share with the universe that no one else can possibly give. And within you is an ever-available, ever-dependable, God-motivated beam-voice, not only to give you accurate guidance, but to tell you everything you need to know about anything you need to know whenever you need to know it. And that automatically makes You greater than anything that can happen to you—now or ever. What more could you ask of Life than that!

So long, my Hearty! Thanks for coming through the book! I know you'll fare well from here on, without having to wish it in your direction, for your great Comrade God goes with you all the way.

CPSIA information can be obtained at www.ICGtesting.com
Printed in the USA
BVOW06s1347300316

442290BV00008B/122/P